PETER HETHERINGTON

D0247727

WHOSE LAND IS OUR LAND?

The use and abuse of Britain's forgotten acres

POLICY PRESS INSIGHTS

First published in Great Britain in 2015 by

Policy Press
University of Bristol
1-9 Old Park Hill
Bristol
BS2 8BB
UK
t: +44 (0)117 954 5940
pp-info@bristol.ac.uk
www.policypress.co.uk

North America office:
Policy Press
c/o The University of Chicago Press
1427 East 60th Street
Chicago, IL 60637, USA
t: +1 773 702 7700
f: +1 773 702 9756
sales@press.uchicago.edu
www.press.uchicago.edu

British Library Cataloguing in Publication Data
A catalogue record for this book is available from the British Library.

Library of Congress Cataloging-in-Publication Data
A catalog record for this book has been requested.

ISBN 978-1-4473-2532-1 (paperback)
ISBN 978-1-4473-2534-5 (ePub)
ISBN 978-1-4473-2535-2 (Mobi)

Cover design by Andrew Corbett
Front cover: image kindly supplied by Getty
Printed and bound in Great Britain by 4edge Limited, Essex
Policy Press uses environmentally responsible print partners

Contents

Photos and sources		iv
Acknowledgements		v
One	Land for all?	1
Two	The people's land?	13
Three	Land denied	25
Four	Land secure?	38
Five	Unclear ownership	55
Six	Land for the people	63
Seven	Villages and neighbourhoods rising	75
Eight	Highlands and Islands rising	81
Nine	Will England rise?	93
Index		105

Photos and sources

Hartside ... "our varied land in microcosm" (Andrew Farrell)   2

Pennine Way: the first long-distance footpath (Peter Hetherington)   5

Wallington Estate's grand house (Peter Hetherington)   19

Sheep safely grazing on National Trust land (Peter Hetherington)   29

Low-lying land in East Anglia (Peter Hetherington)   31

Alnwick Castle (Andrew Farrell)   41

The Duke of Buccleuch and Queensberry (pictured outside Drumlanrig Castle) (Buccleuch Estates)   45

The Duke of Northumberland in the extensive parkland overlooking the Cheviot Hills (Peter Hetherington)   50

Wind turbines on the Ellington Estate (Peter Hetherington)   57

Affordable and private housing under construction at Crosby Ravensworth, Cumbria (Peter Hetherington)   69

Community land trust development (Peter Hetherington)   76

Scottish coastline (Peter Hetherington)   83

After the kill: deer stalking in the Highlands (Murdo Macleod)   87

Island of Eigg (Murdo Macleod)   89

The population of Eigg is rising (Murdo Macleod)   90

Hadrian's Wall path (Peter Hetherington)   96

Flood defences in East Anglia (Peter Hetherington)   97

Acknowledgements

Sometime in the 1970s, the late chairman of the former Highlands and Islands Development Board railed against the 'unacceptable face of feudalism'. It was a time of great uncertainty for people whose livelihood depended on estates in northern Scotland. Ownership was sometimes hotly contested as holdings were broken up and assets stripped, with little, if any, consideration for the inhabitants. As Scottish correspondent for *The Guardian*, reporting these events, it led to a growing fascination with our land. On long car journeys up north from our (then) Edinburgh home, our daughters – Laura and Mairi – would point towards hill, loch or distant island and ask: "Who owns all that?" I would make an attempt to answer. It became a game.

So began a longer journey, writing occasionally about land, plodging across moorland and mountain to record the vagaries of ownership. Moving south, the fascination grew. However, journalists depend on the knowledge and guidance of others to turn ideas into – hopefully – something readable. So, grateful thanks to Professor Philip Lowe, of Newcastle University's Centre for Rural Economy, for his encouragement, support and wise counsel. Kate Henderson and Hugh Ellis, Chief Executive and Policy Director of the Town and Country Planning Association, respectively, deserve special thanks for their valuable insights. George Dunn, Chief Executive of the Tenant Farmers' Association, has been a font of considerable knowledge. Ditto many others. In addition, the late Professor Sir Peter Hall was immensely generous with his time, and wisdom. Special thanks to the estimable Murdo Macleod, photographer extraordinary, for permission to use his superb Highlands and Islands photographs. Andrew Farrell proved invaluable with photographic help.

Many thanks also to Policy Press – Emily Watt, Laura Vickers and others – for their enthusiasm and support.

Thanks and love, most of all, to Christine for both putting up with me and joining me on the journey. Much love to Laura, Mairi, Andrew and Craig – and to Dominic, Hamish, Wilbur and Edie as they discover our glorious land.

ONE

Land for all?

This land is your land
This land is my land
From the Downs to the Western Highlands
From the oak wood forest to the Lakeland waters
This land was made for you and me.[1]

To reach the summit of the Hartside Pass, high in the North Pennines, is to marvel at the rich tapestry that is the British landscape: our land. From this Cumbrian vantage point, you can view prime pasture, marginal upland, mountain top and forested fell-side, moorland, wide estuary, and adjoining coastal plains on the English and Scottish sides of the Solway Firth. The spirits can be lifted, the inner soul replenished, by the infinite variety on offer in this slice of our land – to which we can surely claim a moral, if not a legal, right as UK citizens.

No other place in a small island offers such a panoramic sweep across England and into Scotland: two nations broadly sharing a system of ownership that, in some areas, has remained relatively unchanged for centuries. But for how much longer?

Below the immediate summit of Hartside, one of the highest roads in England, the rich dairy farmland of the Eden valley rolls into the

Hartside ... "our varied land in microcosm" – England and Scotland –
below the summit (Source: Andrew Farrell)

extensive holdings of one of the country's oldest aristocracies – the
Lowthers – stretching back to the 11th century and the subsequent
largesse of Edward I. It provides a lush, pastoral foreground to the
majestic peaks of the Lake District westwards, the ultimate summit
of England, which incorporates the biggest single chunk of land
owned by the UK's largest conservation and membership charity, the
National Trust.

The spectacular view from the Hartside summit – for me, the most
varied, breathtaking vista in Britain – reveals not only our island in
microcosm, but also the concentrated pattern of landownership that
has long characterised Britain, briefly disturbed by an English civil
war in the 17th century. It provides a starting point to raise several
questions about our land, and the true value we place upon it beyond
the sometimes obscene monetary gain from either trading it or using
it as a shelter from taxation (of which more later).

When our island – particularly England – faces the challenges of sustaining a growing population, it is surely reasonable to ask why the UK government has no active land policy to address the pressures of feeding, watering and housing the population as climate change, and rising sea levels, threaten our most productive acres.[2] Land has rarely been a more valuable commodity for the super-rich. Our rural acres are now seen as a safer investment than prime central London property and gold,[3] with little, if any, fiscal measures to curb current trading excesses and, hopefully, bring down the cost of land for housing and for farming.

So obsessed are governments with the whims of the 'free market' (free for whom?) that we seem to have lost any sense of proportion. We are, at best – assuming we even consider the pressures on our land – locked into a cycle of despair, of inevitability, a 'Why bother?' mentality that precludes any sensible intervention in the interests of all the people. It was not always like this.

Beyond the moral, if not the legal, interest (stake?) that we all have in our land as citizens of the UK's diverse nations, it is useful to ponder one glaring contradiction: while society has changed immeasurably during the 20th century and into the 21st, the ownership of our land remains remarkably concentrated. This, as we shall see, is in spite of a transfer in ownership from the big landed estates to former tenant farmers in the 1920s and 1930s, heavy taxation viewed as 'penal' by the aristocracy during that period, and the vague post-war commitment – never realised – for the public ownership of our land. As the geographer Professor Richard Munton[4] has noted, of the 80+ per cent of rural land owned by private individuals, family trusts and corporations, 'a significant proportion remains in the hands of a few owners'.

At first sight, the roll-call of ownership appears diverse. Let us start with the UK government, through the Forestry Commission (2.2 million acres) – the biggest single landowner of all; then the National Trust in England, Wales and Northern Ireland (620,000 acres), underpinned by specific legislation; followed by the Ministry of Defence (568,000 acres); pension funds, hedge funds and utilities (about 600,000 acres); the Crown Estate, a semi-state body (343,000 acres); and the Royal Family directly (257,000 acres).[5]

That tells only part of the story. Throw in the old aristocracy, like the Duke of Buccleuch and Queensberry (240,000 acres, mainly in Scotland) and his cousin just across the border – the Duke of Northumberland (130,000 acres) – and a fair slice of the UK is still owned by successors to a line of the old rich, given vast tracts of land as grace and favours by successive monarchs, sometimes stretching back a thousand years.

On one level, the landed class might no longer appear a significant political and economic force; House of Lords reform in 1999, after all, consigned hereditary peers to history (Margaret Thatcher had five significant landowners in a cabinet of 16). Yet, on another level, this class, as we shall see, still wields power and influence in counties, communities and property markets, sometimes by using their extensive holdings as a platform to create domestic and international development companies underpinned by valuable real estate empires in London, the shires and elsewhere.

But what of the countryside itself? It is a question rarely asked, but one that should be addressed. Few appreciate that it has changed significantly over the centuries, particularly since the early 20th century. From the borderlands, to the Highlands and Islands of Scotland, to the flatlands of Eastern England, and to the downlands of the South, our small island offers a rich variety of landscapes, invariably portrayed as timeless – although, in reality, they are often anything but changeless.

Rural Britain, as the academic and historian Howard Newby has emphasised, holds a special place in our affections – largely because we draw from it a sense of our history and culture, 'our very identity as a nation'.[6] Certainly, the wide open spaces of our land nourish the inner soul, providing both solace, inspiration, exercise and recreation in 15 protected national parks, 46 Areas of Outstanding Natural Beauty (AONBs), countless nature reserves, 11,000 miles of coastline, 137,000 miles of rights of way in England and Wales – supplemented by freedom to roam on countless additional acres – and relatively open access in Scotland.

Pennine Way: the first long-distance footpath, 268 miles long, conceived after 1945 in a raft of progressive countryside and planning legislation now being whittled away

We romanticise our countryside through the work of great artists, poets, composers: Constable, Scottish Colourists, Wordsworth, Burns, Vaughan Williams, Delius, for instance. However, while we draw so much from our land, physically and mentally, paradoxically, many of us take its timeless qualities – often imagined more than real – for granted. We farm it, although well-short of providing self-sufficiency in basic crops – indeed, home-grown food production is falling – and it is a safe bet that few realise that our most productive agricultural area, in Eastern England, is most susceptible to climate change, with 57% of our best agricultural land at or below sea level.[7]

We build on land, although insufficiently to match household formation with housing need. We exploit it for energy, through wind turbines, heat pumps and hydro-power. We draw water from land, although in the most populated areas of the South-East and East of England, demand falls short of supply. We grow trees on it for a variety of uses. We exploit it for minerals, and might soon turn to hydraulic fracturing, or 'fracking', to recover oil and gas from shale rock well below farmland – although the Government's ambition to tap this controversial resource is meeting strong local opposition from protesters and councils, fearing unquantified environmental damage.

Taking a cue from those romantic poets, some have even suggested that we draw something extra from our land, subconsciously going beyond aesthetic appreciation, the nice view. Thus, it lifts our spirits, reinforces our national identities – English, Scottish or Welsh – and enhances our physical, mental and spiritual well-being through a closeness to nature, the antidote to urban Britain.[8]

In truth, ministers across successive UK governments have failed to formulate an active policy that truly values land in its multiplicity of uses beyond the considerable speculative monetary gains fuelled by what accountants casually call 'tax efficiency' – 'avoidance' in everyday language – and seeks to both protect and exploit our most basic resource. Balancing competing interests is a tough call. However, if we are to nourish and house Britain, an active land policy must somehow top the political agenda once again. Bluntly, we are in danger of wasting our most precious resource through a combination of government inaction and collective indifference – in sharp contrast to a combination of both active government and progressive civil society in the first half of the 20th century, as noted in Chapter Two.

Britain is invariably portrayed as a small, crowded island, with little room for more housing, let alone the new towns and communities that the country needs to meet rapid household formation. It is a great misconception perpetuated by an anti-development lobby driven by 'nimby-ism' and fuelled by well-funded countryside groups – and for a period during the life of the 2010–15 UK government, also by the National Trust, which assumed a campaigning role out of step with some of its members.

Like the poets, this lobby romanticises a countryside seemingly preserved in aspic for centuries, below lurid headlines of a green and pleasant land under threat from bulldozer, brick and breeze block. The claim of Britain, particularly England, being 'concreted over' is driven purely by emotion. But it has had an impact: opinion polls suggest that most people think that between a quarter and a half of the country is under concrete.[9] In reality, 6% of the 60 million acres that comprise the UK is urbanised, rising to 10% in England. Probably a little over 4% is occupied by housing.

We can argue endlessly about the green – or the grey – dividing line between 'urban' and 'rural', of what constitutes the 'developed' and 'undeveloped', the 'natural' and 'artificial'. However, can we really contend that our 40 million acres of rural land is, in reality, as 'undeveloped' as some countryside and amenity groups maintain?

Take just six examples: the massive drainage of those East Anglian Fens, which began in earnest in the 17th century under the expertise of the Dutch-born engineer Cornelius Vermunden, in order to create England's most productive farming area; intensive farming, driven by the heavy use of pesticides and fertilisers, and the removal of hedgerows in order to deliver large field systems; intrusive forestry plantations, characterised by serried ranks of fast-growing (North American) sitka spruce, sometimes obscuring ancient woodland; mineral extraction, from ugly opencast coal-mining to large-scale quarrying for sand and gravel; and even relatively intensive sheep-grazing in the Lake District, which has significantly changed the landscape since Wordsworth's day in the 18th–19th century, when the fells had a quite different hue.

All of this raises a serious question, rarely discussed, about a countryside often labelled as 'unchanging' but that, in truth, has changed beyond recognition in relatively recent history. Howard Newby,[10] for one, has questioned whether our idyllic image of rural Britain matches the reality:

> The countryside may be the repository of our 'heritage', but it is often the countryside of tower silos (beside farms), asbestos barns, uprooted hedgerows, ploughed-up moorland, burning stubble, pesticides, factory farming … sometimes our idyllic image stops us seeing reality.

Perhaps that romantic, emotional attachment – harking back to a mythical past of quaint villages, contented farm workers and an orderly countryside – has grown with our transformation from a largely rural to an overwhelmingly urban society, particularly from the mid- to late 19th century. This conveniently sidesteps the reality of a workforce often surviving in hand-to-mouth conditions, and effectively forced from the countryside as landless labourers during the Enclosures (of which more later).

Just over 150 years ago, all land was owned by 4.5% of the population. The rest owned nothing. The turnaround since could be called a quiet revolution, certainly a social phenomenon: the rapid rise of property ownership over the last 50 years, boosted by the cut-price sale of almost two million council houses – and now the prospect of a government-enforced sale of some of the 1.3 million housing association properties in England – has given approaching 70% of the population a small stake in the country. Ironically, the level of home ownership fell under the 2010–15 Conservative-led government, with renting becoming the tenure of necessity, if not of choice, for many younger people priced out of the market. That is hardly a triumphal legacy for a party that once saw itself as the natural party of home ownership.[11]

However, those who comprise the late Lady (Margaret) Thatcher's fabled 'home-owning democracy' account for a tiny slice of the land mass – and beyond their small plots, many up to now have probably cared little about either the ownership of land or, more importantly, the use to which our 60 million acres are put. Could the mood be changing, particularly in Scotland? In her first move as leader of the Scottish National Party in late November 2014, First Minister Nicola Sturgeon, a feisty west of Scotland lawyer, invoked social democracy as her political watchwords and made 'radical action on land reform' a centrepiece of her legislative programme for government. However, she denied that this constituted 'class warfare' and she said that responsible landowners should be 'valued and respected'.[12]

On land policy, as in so many other policy areas, England and Scotland are slowly pulling apart. The Scottish government's ambition to update existing land reform legislation (already making it easier for communities to acquire big estates) is seen by the Duke of Buccleuch, and other landowners, as a looming threat to their extensive holdings.

As we shall see, he questions the very survival of the family enterprises in Scotland and speaks of a 'huge amount of uncertainty ... a tipping point'.[13] Could Scotland, then, be leading a relatively peaceful land reform revolution across Britain? Up to now, in the distinctly different political environment of Westminster, reform in England is not on the agenda of any major party – in the first half of the last century, it was a burning issue – although some landowners fear that the waves from the Scottish government's rural agenda will begin rippling across the border.

However, even a modest suggestion from one leading rural academic for an informal charter between the state and landowners, setting out rights and responsibilities, has so far fallen on deaf ears.[14] The Department for Environment, Food and Rural Affairs (Defra) in England, which, as its name implies, should have a wide-ranging brief embracing land in general – its use, abuse, condition, potential and ownership – seems to have abandoned any pretence of being a powerful player. Defra is low down in the Whitehall pecking order. It suffered bigger cuts than most departments during the 2010–15 Conservative-led government (£500 million) and must find £300 million in savings by 2016.[15] Funding for flood defences, essential for protecting our most productive farmland, took a big hit before being partially restored after devastating floods in the South-West of England early in 2014. They were preceded by exceptional tidal surges on the east coast late in 2013. We have been warned! But where is the long-term plan?

Here is the leading question: do we use land for the benefit of all our citizens or for a privileged few? A select group, after all, exploit land for personal, and institutional, gain – pushing up its value to such dizzying levels that, in the 10 years to 2014 alone, the average selling price for arable land in England increased by 277% (in the previous decade, prices rose by just 41%).[16] Even that is overshadowed by sharp-eyed speculators who make millions from land if they are lucky enough to get planning permission for new development and then selling it on for building. This raises prices further to eye-watering levels – around £1 million an acre at its peak before 2007/08, and currently up to £500,000 – making home-ownership a distant dream for those on average incomes. Through this speculation, land can account for two thirds of the cost of a new home in parts of Britain.[17] However, if communities are clever and circumstances allow, they can acquire small parcels from benevolent landowners for village and neighbourhood benefit – affordable homes, for instance – thus reaping rewards of an uplift in value to help a growing number of community land trusts sprouting in England.

To answer the question 'Whose land is our land?' is to invite a string of seemingly contradictory answers. In some countries, where a republican constitutional settlement is built on the back of a revolution, the answer seems barely worth asking. It is, in part at least, the people's land through either varied owner-occupation or the direct involvement of either local or national government (lest we forget, currently, the biggest UK landowner of all). As the geographer Richard Munton has argued, there is now a general acceptance that rights in land constitute a social relation – whether material, ideological or symbolic – while the distinction between 'public' and 'private' interests has become blurred.[18]

To dig deeper, we need to go back in history, to when landownership was an emotive issue; it was certainly a deeply political one through the 19th century and into 20th centuries, when the old aristocracy, with good reason, felt threatened by the state. Moreover, in Scotland, at least, history seems to be repeating itself.

Notes

[1] Guthrie, W. (1940) 'This land is our land'. Lyrical British derivation by folk duo Chris Ellis and Rosie Toll. Chris credits Billy Bragg for a fuller, lyrically different, recorded version, see: www.politicalfolkmusic.org/wordpress/billy-bragg-this-land-is-your-land

[2] Foresight (2010) *Land use futures: making the most of our land in the 21st century*, London: Government Office for Science. Available at: www.gov.uk/government/collections/land-use-futures

[3] Daneshka, S. (2015) 'UK farm land returns more than Mayfair', *Financial Times*, 18 February. Available at: www.ft.com

[4] Munton, R., 'Rural land ownership in the United Kingdom: changing patterns and future possibilities for land use', Land Use Policy. Available at: www.elsevier.com/locate/landusepol

[5] Cahill, K. (2011) 'The great property swindle', *New Statesman*, 7 March. Available at: www.newstatesman.com

[6] Newby, H. (1988) *The countryside in question*, Hutchinson.

[7] Foresight (2010) *Land use futures: making the most of our land in the 21st century*, London: Government Office for Science. Available at: www.gov.uk/government/collections/land-use-futures

[8] Winter, M. and Lobley, M. (2009) *What is land for?*, Earthscan.

[9] Ipsos Mori survey for British Property Federation (2012). Available at: www.ipsos-mori.com/Assets/Docs/Polls/SRI_IpsosMORIBPFtopline_080512.PDF. See also Cahill, K. (2011) 'The great property swindle', *New Statesman*, 7 March. Available at: www.newstatesman.com

[10] Newby, H. (1988) *The countryside in question*, Hutchinson.

[11] *Financial Times* (2015) 'UK housing inequality grows as generation gap in ownership widens', 25 February. Available at: www.ft.com

[12] Sturgeon, N. (2014) 'Business has nothing to fear', *Financial Times*, 30 November. Available at: www.ft.com

[13] Scott, R., Duke of Buccleuch and Queensberry, interviewed October 2014, at Bowhill, Scottish Borders.

[14] Hetherington, P. (2011) 'Whose land is it anyway?', *Modus,* monthly Royal Institution of Chartered Surveyors magazine, May.

[15] See: www.bbc.co.uk/news/science-environment-25623157

[16] Daneshka, S. (2015) 'UK farm land returns more than Mayfair', *Financial Times*, 18 February. Available at: www.ft.com

[17] Allen, K. (2015) 'Mind the housing gap', *Financial Times*, 14 March.

[18] Munton, R. (2009) 'Rural land ownership in the United Kingdom: changing patterns and future possibilities for land use', *Land Use Policy*, vol 26, S 1, pp S54-S61. Available at: www.elsevier.com/locate/landusepol

TWO

The people's land?

Now into one a hundred fields are thrown
Their tenants banished, and their pleasure flown![1]

Community ownership, cooperation, empowerment: all these might seem a throwback to another, collectivist age, when land was seen as a resource for all to share – somewhere to grow food, graze animals, plant trees, collect firewood, draw water and, at times, seek inspiration. However, as outlined later, resourceful communities in Scotland and, to some extent, in England are taking some of these values into a modern setting through either outright community ownership of large estates or through targeted community land trusts. From the Highlands and Islands, to Oxfordshire, Devon and Cumbria, they are delivering affordable housing, new businesses and community facilities, driven by need rather than by greed – using land as a vital resource against which they can borrow and build, with the added collateral of communities sometimes buying shares in local trusts to unleash development.

Many people, of course, once had a small a stake in land, however informal. In a small corner of England, they still do. While part of our landscape has been transformed by industrial-scale farming, forestation and mineral extraction, little has changed on five hundred acres at Laxton, in North Nottinghamshire, since the early 17th century; plots are neatly laid out in long strips on open fields, tended lovingly by 18 smallholders and farmers.[2]

This is the only part of Britain to have survived one of the most turbulent periods of rural history: the Enclosures. Through the 17th, 18th and 19th centuries, millions of acres of open fields – on which rural workers had commoners' rights for grazing and growing – were appropriated and enclosed in a long series of parliamentary acts, forcing the poor off the land. Laxton, ironically now owned by the Crown Estate – a big property, landownership and trading business, technically belonging to the reigning monarch 'in right of the Crown' – has thus become a testament to a forgotten way of life.

Everything is neatly detailed on an elaborate estate map – a valuable work of art evoking a rural idyll of haymaking, harvesting, oxen, sheep and contented workers – now held at the University of Oxford's Bodleian library. It was produced by a cartographer, Mark Pierce, in 1635, for the then owner, Sir William Courten, a merchant made rich from East Indian trade.

These open-field systems stretched back to medieval times, when much of England and Wales was common land. As Kate Ashbrook recorded in 2015 for the 150th anniversary of the Open Spaces Society: 'Much of England and Wales was once common ... required to be left to the commoners, but little was.'[3] Soon, of course, enclosed land – appropriated by the powerful – assumed a bigger monetary value and became a commodity. It could be bought, sold, inherited or bequeathed, thus conferring even more power, status and wealth on owners. Today, this is underlined with agricultural land prices reaching such dizzying heights that aspiring farmers – outlined in Chapter Three – are priced out of the market by an elite seeking advantageous tax havens to offload spare millions.

In the run-up to the Enclosures, of course, common land was viewed as inefficient by an acquisitive ruling and landed class, which saw great potential for expanding already substantial estates. With that expansion would come even more power, prestige and, of course, capital appreciation from an emerging market economy and a valuable traded commodity, which is, of course, a finite resource: our land.

Even today, opinion on the reasoning behind the Enclosures is divided. The writer and land reform campaigner Kevin Cahill is in no doubt that the various enclosure acts in the 17th, 18th and 19th centuries – 'decided in favour of the peerage by the peerage' – demonstrated the 'irreversible nature of the change in both power and ownership in Britain'.[4] Our land thus became *their* land.

According to Cahill, the Enclosures were particularly invidious because the aristocracy took from a weak monarchy 'rights which were really those of the common people ... at a time when the common people had neither representation nor power'. In one estimate, 6 million acres of land, a quarter of all cultivated acreage, were appropriated from the second quarter of the 18th century to the first quarter of the 19th, 'mainly by the politically dominant landowners', according to the academic and writer Raymond Williams.[5] He records a long process of 'conquest and seizure ... the land gained by killing, by repression, by political bargains'.

While acknowledging the justifiable grievances of those who lost common grazing land to rich individuals, Peter Clery,[6] with a background in banking and land management, argues that the Enclosures are a subject of 'misunderstanding and sometimes misplaced emotional concern'. He loftily contends that the advantages of consolidating strips into workable holdings 'must have been obvious to the meanest intelligence ... enclosures were essential ... for increased food production to meet the needs of a growing (urban) population'.

However, Dr Hugh Ellis, Director of Policy at the Town and Country Planning Association, is quite clear that agricultural modernisation should not have led to the dispossession of people's land rights, and in Scotland, evicting people from their homes in the infamous Highland Clearances, when thousands were removed by rapacious landlords to make way for sheep.

In their book, *Rebuilding Britain: planning for a better future*,[7] Hugh Ellis and Kate Henderson remind us that the enclosure of common land dispossessed tens of thousands of poor rural workers of their livelihoods – and by the 1870s, after the final Enclosure Act, the idea of collective land rights in Britain had been largely extinguished. The repercussions from these 'legal' land-grabs undoubtedly influenced a radical, reforming Liberal Chancellor of the Exchequer (and subsequent Prime Minister) David Lloyd George in the early 20th century. His 1910 People's Budget hit the landed gentry with land taxes in order to pay for an emerging welfare state. Land reform was high on his agenda – just at it is today in a Scottish government led by social-democrat-inclined First Minister, Nicola Sturgeon.

However, it took almost 80 years after the last Enclosure Act to gain democratic control over land use – falling short of the full-scale public ownership of land initially promised by the Labour Party – through the groundbreaking Town and Country Planning Act 1947, which effectively 'nationalised' the right to develop land. This was a key element of the post-war settlement – whittled away by the 2010–15 Conservative-led government – which delivered a National Health Service, a welfare state, national parks, a substantial footpath network in England and Wales with the same legal status as a highway, and much else.

As the late geographer Sir Peter Hall[8] argued, it is difficult to comprehend in today's political climate the intense emotions surrounding land over the last two decades of the 19th century as repercussions from the enclosures resonated throughout England: 'Essentially, it represented a struggle for power between the old landed classes … and new interests who wanted to dismantle the social influence of the landed estates', he wrote in 2014, shortly before his death.

British agriculture was in crisis at the time, beset by a series of poor harvests and overseas competition from new markets in the Americas and Australasia, for instance. Farm rents were declining as a result, cereal acreage was dramatically down and one landowner, the Duke of Marlborough, remarked in 1885 that half the land would be put on the market, if there was demand – there was not.

Perhaps unsurprisingly, demand for land reform was growing; a Land Nationalisation Society was formed in 1881, producing many pamphlets – although, as Hall observed, the very term 'nationalisation' covered a wide political spectrum, from outright compulsory purchase to progressive nationalisation of all land for the community. Some suggested, with perhaps undue idealism, that a plentiful supply of rural plots would persuade city-dwellers to flock back to the land.

Ebenezer Howard was a practical idealist. Born in London, he had spent four years in the US as a pioneer farmer and later as a shorthand writer in Chicago. Returning to London, a city buzzing with a new radicalism, he began to focus on land. With prices depressed, it was a good time to test his idealism, and so the 'garden city' ideal was born – a near-utopian plan for a self-contained community with high-quality houses, each with a plot for growing food, and with jobs on the doorstep. It has proved enduring, albeit on a smaller scale than Howard envisaged.[9]

Today, it has found favour with all main political parties as one means of solving an acute shortage of housing, particularly in the South-East and East of England, though it is far from clear whether they have signed up to the Howardian ideal of capturing the increase in land values that development creates for the benefit of the community. Collectivism, after all, has largely disappeared from the political lexicon. However, its ethos underpins Letchworth Garden City, in Hertfordshire – Howard's ultimate creation, and forerunner to 28 subsequent new towns – which remains a vibrant community of 33,000. It has an asset base of property and land valued at £130 million, which, in turn, delivers £10 million annually for community benefit.

Howard's idealism chimed with a 'back to the land' theme taken up by a Liberal government, elected in 1906. Some ministers wanted to promote smallholdings for the many landless labourers as a first step on the housing ladder; today, as we shall see, the challenge of getting more younger people onto that ladder, with the average age of farmers estimated at well over 60, is still proving elusive for many aspirants.

However, unlike today, this was a time of considerable activism. The radical housing campaigner and social reformer Octavia Hill – one of the founders of the National Trust in 1895, legally embedded with special legislation in 1907 – was another practical idealist. The

Trust emerged from her passion, a 'fundamental conviction that the poor deserved equal cultural and aesthetic opportunities as the rich', according to the historian Tristram Hunt.[10]

On one level, she might well approve of today's organisation, which has undoubtedly helped to open up the countryside for recreation, while maintaining its 627,000 varied acres of mountain moor and farmland and 775 miles of coastline to a generally high standard, with the help of several thousand tenants and volunteers. Thus, it provides a level of countryside access, and of stewardship, the envy of many other countries.

With 4.2 million members, the Trust also has around 215 grand mansions and houses, splendid gardens, and estates, alongside 40 castles, around 80 nature reserves and much else. However, less well-known is its role as a substantial landlord, with 5,000 housing tenants and 1,800 tenant farmers (including 800 on largish farms), who manage 80% of its land. As we shall see, relations with some of these tenants have been, at best, challenging.[11] Perhaps under pressure, the Trust now appears to be changing course, promising to spend £100 million annually over the next 10 years on the conservation of its houses, gardens and countryside, while developing ways of managing land on a large scale to 'benefit farmers, the economy and the environment'.[12]

A year after the National Trust Act 1907, Lloyd George, similarly infused with radicalism, became Chancellor of the Exchequer, in charge of the finances of Britain and (then) pre-partition Ireland. Passions were running high. Land became a defining political issue in his subsequent People's Budget. Tories were aghast at his taxation proposals: a rise in income tax, a super-tax on incomes over £5,000 and increased death duties, for instance. A Liberal colleague, and former Prime Minister, Lord Rosebery, dismissed the reforms as 'pure socialism', claiming that the budget should be renamed a 'revolution'. The landed class concurred. Lloyd George was unmoved.

As Britain's biggest private landowner, the present Duke of Buccleuch and Queensberry underlines a sense of betrayal, and bitterness, still lingering in the old aristocracy over 100 years later:

Wallington Estate's grand house, donated to the National Trust by former Labour cabinet minister Sir Charles Trevelyan because of his disdain for private land ownership

The balance of power in Britain would be transformed ... effectively stripping the hereditary peerage of its political power ... embarking on a new era of heavy, and ultimately penal taxation that would put paid to many old families and their traditional lands.[13]

Amid the political ferment, one thing eventually became clear: Britain would rarely again experience such a radical passion to reform land (and landlordism), though the Scottish government's current legislative proposals – strengthening pioneering land reform legislation delivered by a Labour–Liberal Democrat Scottish government in 2003 – mark the first attempt in over 100 years to address ownership and the common good.[14] The post-war Labour government, while briefly flirting with full land nationalisation, backed away from radical reform. Now, the Town and Country Planning Act 1947 in England, which delivered control of development on our land – seen as a precursor to public ownership – has been whittled down beyond recognition by a 2010–15 Conservative-led Coalition government committed to creating a smaller state.

The reformist interwar years also proved a turning point in the long campaign for wider access to the mountains, moors and wilderness areas of Britain. Frustrated that so much of our land, often devoted to field sports, was effectively out of bounds for the urban masses seeking fresh air and recreation, a large group of activists from Manchester brought matters to a head in April 1932. They staged a 'mass trespass' at Kinder Scout, in the Peak District – for landowners and the British establishment, the ultimate act of civil disobedience – and clashed with gamekeepers (more accurately, vice versa!). Five of the protesters were arrested, charged with unlawful assembly and breach of the peace, and jailed. Their action, and harsh treatment, provoked a national outcry.

While it proved a defining moment in a long battle for a legal 'right to roam' in the countryside, it took another 68 years to fully realise the full fruits of their labours. They were finally enshrined in England's Countryside and Rights of Way Act 2000, which delivered relatively free access with the publication of new maps showing open areas. However, there was a more immediate impact.

Ministers in the post-1945 Labour government – such as the Chancellor of the Exchequer, Hugh Dalton – were determined to build on the legacy of the 'mass trespass' movement. The result was truly far-reaching legislation, embodied in the National Parks and Access to the Countryside Act 1949. It gave 137,000 miles of footpaths in England and Wales the legal status of highways ('*rights* of way' meant exactly that!), laid the foundations for long-distance national trails (such as the 268-mile Pennine Way) and created 13 national parks (two more were created much later in Scotland). Significantly, the first national park – doubtless in recognition of the Kinder Scout 'mass trespass' – was designated in the Peak District, followed closely by the Lake District.

Interviewing Lady (Barbara) Castle in 2001, a year before her death aged 91, she vividly recalled the 'mass trespasses' in her formative political years, shortly after becoming an MP in 1945. They clearly still aroused a lingering sense of injustice, particularly after walking alongside Dalton in the Northern Pennines and encountering 'keep out' signs, which particularly irritated the one-time Chancellor. Lady Castle recalled: 'These lads and lasses after 1945 said "what were we fighting for if we can't get access to our own countryside?"' She railed: 'The landowners were selfish and self-centred. The working class coming from the industrial areas were clearly the enemy.'[15]

In England, during the ideological climate of 2010–15 – the mindless deconstruction of the planning system; the abolition of regional and national 'quangos'; sidelining the Department of the Environment, Food and Rural Affairs; and scrapping the post of rural advocate, charged with advising the government, as a 'critical friend', on all aspects of the (English) countryside – the wide-ranging reforms of Lloyd George appear audacious. He laid the foundations for the first rural development commission, finally abolished by the 2010–15 Conservative-led government, as well as the Forestry Commission, now the UK's biggest landowner, which narrowly avoided privatisation in the early stages of the last government after it was forced to shelve sell-off proposals following a public outcry from countryside groups. Whether it remains secure in public ownership is an open question. Some fear that the threat of partial privatisation, at least, is on the horizon. The Unite trade union, representing forestry workers, has warned that the UK government might still be 'paving the way' for a forest sell-off.[16]

Lloyd George matched his fierce rhetoric with a passion for delivery rare in contemporary politicians. Today, it is significant that the outcry from the landed classes in Scotland over the Scottish government's determination to push through another round of land reform represents, in many ways, a rerun of the arguments deployed by the aristocracy to attack Lloyd George's rural agenda. His abiding question – 'Who made 10,000 people owners of the land and the rest of us trespassers in the land of our birth?' – still has resonance. In this context, the comments of Scotland's First Minister, Nicola Sturgeon, in

November 2014 are worth recording: 'Scotland's land must be an asset that benefits the many, not the few', she told the Scottish Parliament.[17]

Financial pressure was bearing down on the big estates after the First World War: by 1919, for instance, death duties were increased to 40% on estates worth over £2 million. Partly as a result, the country would soon see the biggest shift in landownership since the dissolution of the monasteries in the 16th century. A combination of high taxation, rising land prices and battlefield slaughter resulted in such a massive transfer of land that, by 1939, owner-occupied farmers held over half of all the agricultural acres.[18] However, many aristocrats still held on to substantial holdings, sometimes by selling outlying portions, mineral rights and other areas for development. Furthermore, in consolidating their estates, they have still managed to remain a powerful force in swathes of Britain.

As Arthur Marwick[19] notes in his study of British society and the First World War:

> The frequent deaths in battle of young aristocrats made the burden of death duties even greater than it otherwise might have been … land values had greatly risen, while rents had not: by selling, the landowner could put the increased value straight into his pocket … they emerged … still in residence in their country seats, with their territorial empires considerably reduced, but with their incomes … probably much healthier than they had been for many years.

Moreover, as I shall argue in Chapter Four, the influence of the old landed class, albeit exercised discreetly, remains strong in some areas.

Throughout the 1930s, land reform remained an issue – not always a burning one – for the Labour Party. Clement Attlee, the future prime minister, who came from a family of Surrey corn merchants, even declared in 1937 that his party 'stood for the national ownership of land'. Labour's post-war manifesto took up the theme, committing the party to 'working towards' land nationalisation.

However, as the historian David Kynaston[20] points out, nationalisation was effectively off the agenda. Instead, with a new Agriculture Act 1947 guaranteeing farm prices, it became 'jackpot time' for many farmers. With this new subsidy regime foreshadowing an era of industrialised farming, the landscape of rural Britain began to change in pursuit of a remorseless goal of maximising production – and, as Kynaston notes, all against the illusion that the character of rural Britain would be unaffected.

Farming, thus, became a powerful lobby. Post-war Labour became its friend; on leaving office, Tom Williams, Attlee's Minister of Agriculture, was even given a small dinner party at Claridges Hotel by a grateful Duke of Norfolk! Today, with the Department for the Environment, Food and Rural Affairs – successor to the old Ministry of Agriculture, Fisheries and Food – a sadly diminished force, it would be hard to imagine any agriculture minister being feted like this.

It might be even harder to imagine a group of activist land reformers, disillusioned about promises surrounding democracy and access to land, setting up their own communities with the aim of creating a cooperative society. They were eventually forced off the land in a violent clash at St George's Hill in Surrey. Their champion, Gerald Winstanley, recorded with some prescience that 'the buying and selling of land, and the fruits on it, one to another, is The cursed thing'.[21] They were The Diggers, and that was the 17th century. Yet, Leon Rosselson's (1974) poem, evoking their struggle, still inspires another generation of activists in Scotland and in England: 'The sin of property we do disdain. No man has any right to buy and sell the earth for private gain.'[22]

Notes

[1] Holloway, W. (1802) 'The Peasants' Fate', English Poetry 1579-1830 Spenser and the Tradition, catalog.hathitrust.org/Record/100613672

[2] See: www.laxtonvisitorcentre.org.uk and www.nottingham.ac.uk/manuscriptsandspecialcollections/learning/laxton/introduction.aspx

[3] Ashbook, K. (2015) *Saving open spaces*, Stroud: Pitkin Publishing and The History Press. Available at: www.thehistorypress.co.uk

[4] Cahill, K. (2002) *Who owns Britain*, Edinburgh: Canongate Books .

[5] Williams, R. (1973) *The country and the city*, Paladin (Chatto and Windus).

[6] Clery, P. (2012) *Green gold: a thousand years of English land*, Andover, Hampshire: Phillimore, p 38.

[7] Ellis, P. and Henderson, K. (2014) *Rebuilding Britain: planning for a better future*, Bristol: Policy Press.

[8] Hall, P. and Ward, C. (2014) *Sociable cities: the 21st-century reinvention of the garden city* (2nd edn), London: Routledge, p 9.

[9] Heritage Foundation, 'Letchworth Garden City', see: www.letchworth.com

[10] Hunt, T., 'Octavia Hill, her life and legacy', *National Trust Magazine* (article 1356393664070). Available at: www.nationaltrust.org.uk

[11] Tenant Farmers' Association, 'National Trust farm and housing tenants share joint concerns', press release 11. Available at: www.tfa.org.uk

[12] See: nationaltrust.org.uk/mag/strategy

[13] Scott, R., Duke of Buccleuch and Queensberry (2012) *Bowhill: the house, its people and its paintings* (ed J.M.D. Scott), Hawick, Scotland: Caique Publishing Ltd, Preface.

[14] Scottish Government (2014) 'The land of Scotland and the common good', report of the Land Reform Review Group. Available at: www.gov.scot/publications/2014/05/2852

[15] Hetherington, P. (2005) 'Upward mobility for all', *The Guardian*, 11 January.

[16] Unite (2015) 'Landworker, fighting for forests and jobs', Spring. Available at: www.unitetheunion.org

[17] See: http://news.scotland.gov.uk/Speeches-Briefings/First-Minister-Programme-for-Government

[18] Clery, P. (2012) *Green gold: a thousand years of English land*, Andover, Hampshire: Phillimore.

[19] Marwick, A. (2006) *The deluge, British society and the First World War* (2nd edn), Palgrave Macmillan.

[20] Kynaston, D. (2007) *Austerity Britain 1945–51*, Bloomsbury.

[21] Town and Country Planning Association, see: www.lovelifeliberty.co.uk

[22] Rosselson, L., see: www.leonrosselson.co.uk

THREE

Land denied

He who works the land will have abundant food,
But he who chases fantasies lacks judgement.[1]

At one time, the sight of a cabinet minister addressing farmers in a room beside a busy auction mart might have attracted just a little publicity – for the exotic setting, if for nothing else. However, such is the status of the Department for the Environment, Food and Rural Affairs (Defra), sidelined on the fringes of government, that few outside the narrow farming world took much interest when its secretary of state spoke at a major farming event.

It was late in 2014 at Hexham, a pleasant Northumberland market town astride a River Tyne rich in salmon. Enter Liz Truss, the third secretary of state for Defra in the five years of the Conservative-led Coalition government (2010–15). While seen as a stopgap when a pedestrian Owen Patterson, a climate-change-cum-EU sceptic on the right of the party, was sacked in July 2014, she continued in her role after the 2015 general election.

Speaking at the Northern Farming Conference, Truss briefly addressed the nub of a dilemma at the heart of farming: namely, attracting younger people into an industry with many elderly farmers.[2] It is a challenge faced by predecessors at Defra, one of whom commissioned a report from a farming specialist, Devon landowner and rural surveyor David Fursdon, early in the life of the 2010–15 government in an attempt to introduce fresh blood into agriculture. By 2013, Fursdon's 'Future of farming review' called for early retirement measures to benefit older farmers, alongside initiatives to encourage new entrants into the industry.[3] It is a major challenge. The report gained little traction. Fursdon, a pragmatic consultant respected across sectors, is, unsurprisingly, frustrated and a little puzzled.

In nearby Somerset, Andrew Fewings knows all about the challenges facing younger people trying to get on to the first rung of an elusive farming ladder.[4] The demand from the young is there all right, he insists; but the supply, in the form of available land – increasingly a speculative plaything for some of the rich – is woefully short. Fewings farms 336 acres, as a tenant of the Crown Estate – a semi-state institution, dating back to 1066, ostensibly owned by the Queen – on the flatlands near Dunster.[5] He concedes that he is relatively lucky; that contemporaries, bent on a farming career, have been much less successful in getting land, albeit to rent.

Ambitious farmers, like the Fewings – Andrew plus wife and business partner Judith – had the odds stacked against them from the outset. Andrew Fewings was a herdsman for 10 years – "working 70–80 hours weekly, saving as much as I could" – before getting the tenancy of a 64-acre county council farm at Trowbridge, Wiltshire, in 1992. Five years later, husband and wife took over the tenancy of another, larger county council farm, near Salisbury; by 1997, they moved to Dunster, where they grow winter wheat on 50 acres to help feed 320 milking cows.

However, a once-extensive national county council farming estate, initiated in the 1920s under the progressive premiership of a radical David Lloyd George, is sadly shrinking. In spite of this, it is still the only route into farming for many young aspirants. The Fewings would love to own their own farm, but they know that it is unlikely with an increasing shortage of suitably priced holdings: "I could possibly manage it, but I'd have to downsize quite a bit ... wouldn't be able to buy many acres", sighs Andrew.

According to Philip Lowe,[6] Professor of Rural Economy at Newcastle University, Britain has 'the most concentrated land ownership in Europe', with an 'unreformed landed class' offering increasingly fewer openings to those interested in entering agriculture. "If a farm like mine comes up for tenancy these days, I reckon you'd get at least 100 applicants", adds Andrew Fewings. Rapidly rising agricultural land prices are further restricting entry into farming: "They just do not reflect what you can earn from the land", bemoans Fewings. "Institutions, people from the City, those with money to spare, are inflating prices, putting land further beyond reach."

Much as Liz Truss, and her predecessors, lament the barriers preventing younger people choosing agriculture as a career – then, hopefully, progressing up the farming ladder – precious little action has been taken since the early 1920s, when Lloyd George introduced legislation allowing county councils to buy estates. Ministers of yesteryear had ambition. It helped, of course, that a land-buying spree under Lloyd George coincided with a period when, unlike today, land prices were initially low in an agricultural depression. His programme chimed with a back-to-the-land movement – underpinned by the Smallholdings Act 1890 – which eventually grew to become an institution offering one of the few ways into agriculture for young people, like the Fewings back in 1992. "But for every generation it now gets harder", sighs Andrew Fewings. "Some councils have been clever, holding onto land and doubled their money in five or so years. But others have seen their farms go as a way to get quick cash."

Although still covering over 200,000 acres across England (in 50 council areas), with over 2,000 tenants, well over 100,000 acres have been sold since the mid-1980s, when the overall county council estate covered 340,000 acres. "We have seen the number of tenants more than halved over 25 years", laments George Dunn, chief executive of the Tenant Farmers' Association (TFA). In spite of this, the TFA's 2020 'Vision for agriculture' report notes that the county farms are still the principal route into farming for new entrants: 'The long-term decline in the number and area … is a major blow to the agricultural industry and the nation's long-term interests', it adds.

As the senior official in charge of Gloucestershire's county council farms for 27 years, Charles Coats has become the national authority on a system that successive governments once saw as a 'gateway' into agriculture – a progression from smallholding to a larger farm. Coats recalls the Agriculture Act 1947, which viewed the farms as a 'ladder of opportunity', and, subsequently, the Agriculture Act 1970, laying down a 'general aim' for councils to acquire more land for aspiring farmers – and, crucially, requiring them to submit annual plans to the government for scrutiny. "But there was no one around to give these plans the necessary critical oversight … they were a discretionary, not a mandatory service, which meant they became very vulnerable", he adds despairingly.[7] Yet, Coats insists that demand is still strong: "I have interviewed a thousand or more applicants over the years and put 400 to 500 into farms and, believe me, most would have been able to operate on bigger farms successfully if they had the opportunity."

Tenant farming, of course, can be a precarious business. Ownership of land, whether private or charitable, is not necessarily a determinant of enlightened landlord–tenant relations – as some of the 1,800-plus farming tenants of the National Trust in England and Wales can attest. Of its 600,000-plus acres, 80% is let to tenants who, according to the official Trust philosophy, 'manage our land in ways that support our environmental and aesthetic aims'.[8] However, relations with some tenants have been so poor that their representative body – the TFA – accused the Trust in 2014 of too often treating tenants as 'rent cheques rather than as true partners'.[9]

One tenant, an award-winning organic farmer who rents 900 acres of upland from the Trust in Northumberland – part of its extensive Wallington Estate – complained that he was subjected to a lengthy, painful, review process that resulted in a 70 per cent rent increase. He is now facing another substantial hike. It has clearly left a lingering bitterness: "Our landlord–tenant relationship has gone", says Simon Bainbridge[10]:

Sheep safely grazing on National Trust land. With 1,800 farming tenants, the Trust is one of the largest agricultural landlords.

"The landlord's only focus is on commercial rental gains, irrespective of the holding's ability to pay that rent. Tenants work with the National Trust to help them achieve their ethos even though this means the productive capacity of the holding may fall – yet, during rent negotiations, the ethos can be pushed to one side, with the Trust taking the position of the hypothetical landlord in order to maximise rent. The days of discussion and negotiation for both parties appears to have gone for the time being, and with that, a relationship which was once positive."

Ironically, the 14,000-acre Wallington Estate, with its grand house and gardens, was given to the Trust by the former Labour cabinet minister Sir Charles Trevelyan in 1941 because of his disdain for private landownership. Not for nothing has the Trust, which has the country's largest tenanted farm operation, been reassessing its land management philosophy and the role of its regional surveyors and agents on the ground. George Dunn, of the TFA, thinks that attitudes might now be changing: "The good thing that's come out of this is that they've recognised they have a problem ... that they are in a bad place ... we have been very critical", he noted. "The heart and soul is beginning to change, but it will take a long time to filter to regional teams and to tenants."[11]

That change was first signalled in March 2015. The Trust launched a 10-year land strategy, costed at £1 billion, to reverse what it called decades of unsustainable land management, intensive farming and loss of habitats, which had sent wildlife numbers tumbling.[12] This came as a surprise to some tenants, who said that they had been farming in a sustainable way – 'ticking all the right environmental boxes', with stewardship schemes to protect wildlife – only to be rewarded with hefty rent increases.

Significantly, the Trust's Director General, Dame Helen Ghosh, is the former top civil servant – officially titled permanent secretary – in Defra. She said that the Trust would work with its tenants to try and make farms more 'sustainable'. However, the *Farmers' Guardian* newspaper quoted farm leaders as saying that her comments were 'ironic' when the Trust's own land agents were 'notorious for hiking up rents for short-term gain'.[13]

Alongside this simmering resentment among some National Trust tenants – strained relationships, frankly more associated in the public mind with private landlordism – lies one ever-present question: Where are the incentives, the active policies in government – rather than the ministerial rhetoric – to create a new 'ladder of opportunity' into farming as land becomes an ever-more valuable traded commodity, with speculators exploiting the most basic resource on which we all depend?

Farm land offers generous tax breaks on inheritance and capital gains tax. It qualifies for agricultural property and business property relief. This means that land is exempt from inheritance tax after two years if it is actively farmed. Moreover, additional relief allows the sale of a farming asset to be rolled into a new farming business. Capital gains tax is thus deferred until the sale of the asset.

According to one of the country's leading farmers, this rampant speculation, fuelled by tax avoidance, is hindering rather than helping what should be a national drive to become more self-sufficient in food production. Poul Hovesen, arable farmer of the year in 2014, utilises sophisticated crop rotation and cultivation techniques to maintain good soil and improve yields on two farms he manages in Norfolk: a 5,000-acre enterprise, north-west of Norwich, and a 7,000-acre operation on the nearby Holkham Estate (of which more shortly). He is appalled by the condition of recently traded farmland, in the South of England, where he thinks that the potential for both maintaining and improving soil – and, hence, raising crop production – is being lost through short-term contract farming.[14]

Low-lying land in East Anglia. Management of flood alleviation and drainage, 'critical to maintaining domestic food production'. But has the message penetrated the government?

Agriculture, as Truss says, is critical to our economy, employing 400,000 people, covering at least 70% of our land and generating £100 billion annually.[15] Indeed, when combined with food production, she maintains that it is Britain's largest manufacturing sector – bigger even than car and aerospace production combined. Why, then, she asked in Hexham, was it seen as unattractive to the young. Why indeed?

Perhaps, on the evidence of both Andrew Fewings and Charles Coats, there is a hidden reservoir of young people, frustrated at the absence of opportunities because of highly concentrated ownership, alongside a speculative marketplace where food production is of secondary importance to tax 'efficiency'. In short, the plea for more young people to enter farming offered few, if any, solutions – worthy, if uninspiring, and woefully weak on delivery.

A few weeks after the Hexham conference, in early 2015, Liz Truss was speaking at the Oxford Farming Conference, the premier event on the agricultural calendar.[16] It is a world away from a functional northern mart, where a post-debate supper among the dreaming spires cost £74, with wine and an 'oxtail club dinner' a mere £42. However, the minister's theme was broadly similar. She noted, again, that farming was a 'sunrise industry', and even suggested that, as a 'high-tech powerhouse', it was at the heart of the government's long-term economic plan and vital to the country's well-being.

This seemed, at first hearing, political progress: a government plan, no less, to address farming and, by implication, food security, with encouragement for younger entrants thrown in for good measure. These two areas are interlinked: farmers are getting older. Consequently – as David Fursdon's shelved report for Defra underlined – they are sometimes hanging on to holdings well past retirement age with no succession plan in place. Perversely, as we have seen, opportunities for new entrants are often few and far between at a time when a new breed of farmers is vital for achieving the seemingly elusive goal of higher production for domestic consumption.

The National Farmers' Union (NFU), guardian of farming interests, has been campaigning for higher domestic food production for several years. In a 2011 report,[17] it highlighted the country's relative vulnerability from an overreliance on unpredictable imports. It is an issue that rarely, if ever, seems to command attention at the higher levels of government, in spite of further warnings in another NFU report for its 2015 annual conference.[18] Today, we are lucky to produce 62% of our own food – down 20% since 1980. While the NFU believes that the country has the potential to reach 85% self-sufficiency, it argues that inadequate productivity and underinvestment in research and development has placed the country behind mainland European counterparts. By 2040, the NFU fears that domestic food production will have fallen by a further 10%. To be fair, as the organic charity the Soil Association has pointed out, the NFU research would carry more weight if its members were not using so much land for growing industrial crops – oilseed rape for biofuels, for instance – at the expense of food production.[19]

According to Poul Hovesen, in Norfolk, the country easily has the potential to become more self-sufficient with better farming management leading to improved soil cultivation: "UK agriculture has stagnated over the past 12 years", he laments.[20] I asked Hovesen, a Dane who came to Britain 28 years ago, whether the current trading market was serving the country well. "No, I don't think it is", he replied after a visit to Hampshire where, he said, fund managers from London were acquiring land. "Do they farm sustainably, do they have a long-term vision?", he asked rhetorically.

In many ways, our current plight is the reverse of a dilemma in the late 19th century, and into the 20th, when land prices were collapsing and agriculture was in depression; a combination of poor harvests and imports from the Americas and Australasia had undermined domestic production. Today, conversely, demand for farming land has been far outstripping supply. In the decade to 2014, prices for prime arable farmland – concentrated especially in East Anglia – rose almost fourfold, by 277%. (In the decade 1994–2004, they grew by 41%.)[21] Prime London property went up by *just* 127% over the same period.

What is driving this massive appreciation? Dr Jason Beedell,[22] head of research at land agents Smiths Gore, does not offer the obvious answer: "It is not particularly related to agricultural commodity prices ... the main driver is supply – put simply, the lack of land to buy", he says. Whereas in the 1970s, for instance, around 500,000 acres went on the market annually – perhaps up to 2% of agricultural land – today, he estimates that only 100,000–150,000 acres change hands each year.

Easy lending is boosting prices. If an investor is lucky enough to find a modest few hundred acres – or, perhaps, several thousand – he or she will have little trouble tapping finance for investment in a finite resource. Land, unlike property, is recession-proof. It defies economic downturns thanks to the European Union's Common Agricultural Policy, which – as discussed in Chapter Six – generously subsidises farmers and landowners (and, hence, land) regardless of the state of the economy. In short, according to Beedell, banks are invariably happy to lend because land is such an appreciating asset; arable land, for instance, is going for around £10,000 an acre, and perhaps £1,000 more with farm buildings. While farmers account for the majority of buyers, they are increasingly having to compete with private investors and institutions – pushing up prices even further, according to Beedell.

When the 40,000-acre farming business of the troubled Cooperative Group went on the market in 2013, fears of a speculative free-for-all were understandably rampant. This, after all, marked the biggest sale of UK farm land in many years. In the event, however, the Wellcome Trust, the world's second-largest medical research charity – which invests extremely wisely – stepped in. It paid £249 million for the business. Not for nothing did the Trust's managing director of investments underscore the importance of the purchase by quoting Mark Twain:[23] 'they are not making any more land'.

Now, another player has moved into the market. Edinburgh-based Greenshields Agri owns 2,860 acres, and farms another 640, on what it calls the 'northern grain belt' between the Humber in England and the Tay in Scotland. In early March 2015, it became the first arable landowner to seek a stock-market listing. Its aim is to raise £3 million to buy more land.[24] Founded in 2010, the company currently farms in both Northumberland and immediately across the border in South-East Scotland. Much of its appeal is the investment potential of British farmland, which it describes as 'the most transparent in Europe'; once farmed for two years, it is, of course, exempt from inheritance tax. A company spokesman said that its shares would probably qualify for exemption. However, with many farmers either approaching or over retirement age – often, according to Greenshields, with no successor in place – the company made a significant further pitch to the middle-aged and elderly: either sell land directly to us or exchange it for shares in Greenshields.

Overall, agriculture accounts for around three quarters of land sales annually, with forests making up for a further 10%. In addition, another 15% of the land sold each year is for development and infrastructure – a tiny proportion of which goes for housing. All of which raises one question? Aside from Greenshields, what does the fortunate buyer do with newly acquired farming land? Invariably, it is rented for agriculture, sometimes to supplement existing farms that need to expand operations; taking up Paul Hovesen's observation, though, this new system – detaching the owner from the use of land – hardly serves the country well.

Large-scale buying, of course, has huge advantages for those with a few million to offload. As George Dunn, chief executive of the TFA, says, this amounts to a "massive state subsidy" for those already enjoying considerable wealth.[25] He asks: "What does the state get back? Not much."

It is a leading question, which few, if any, in the 2010–15 Conservative-led UK government were prepared to answer. However, cross-party exchanges at the Oxford Farming Conference in January 2015 proved revealing. Turning to the English Agriculture Minister, George Eustice – a deputy to Liz Truss – the Scottish government's Cabinet Secretary for Rural Affairs and the Environment, Richard Lochhead,[26] asked: "Our struggle is to make more land available to let. You and your colleagues in (the UK) government could make a difference by taking fiscal measures quickly." The UK government, for the time being, is responsible for most taxation in Scotland, although some tax-raising powers are being devolved to Edinburgh.

Eustice was then asked from the conference floor if the UK government, for instance, had any concerns about the huge land-buying programme undertaken recently by Sir James Dyson, who made his fortune from the bag-less vacuum cleaner. Sir James, who recently bought a 3,000-acre estate in Lincolnshire from the Crown Estate – taking his overall land portfolio to 25,000 acres – has a main home at Dodington Park, an 18th-century manor house in

Gloucestershire. Eustice replied: "Property ownership and property rights are a fundamental of a free market." And that was it.

Rarely are the differences between an English and Scottish minister so publicly exposed. However, for now, both countries share at least one common feature: the continuing dominance of the old aristocracy, the landed class, in large areas – and none more so than in England's most northerly county.

Notes

[1] *Proverbs* (12, v 11). Thanks to George Dunn, chief executive of the Tenant Farmers' Association (TFA).

[2] 'TFA 2020 Vision for agriculture'. Available at: www.tfa.org.uk

[3] Defra (2013) 'Future of farming review'. Available at: www.gov.uk/government/uploads/system/uploads/attachment_data/file/211175/pb13982-future-farming-review-20130709.pdf

[4] Fewings, A., interviewed December 2014.

[5] See: www.thecrownestate.co.uk

[6] Hetherington, P. (2011) 'Whose land is it anyway?', *Modus*, monthly magazine of the Royal Institution of Chartered Surveyors, May.

[7] Coats, C., interviewed December 2014.

[8] See: www.nationaltrust.org.uk/article-1356402501974/

[9] TFA press release no 11, Ref MR11. Available at: www.tfa.org.uk

[10] Bainbridge, S., interviewed December 2014, at Donkin Rigg, Morpeth, Northumberland.

[11] Dunn, G., interviewed February 2015.

[12] National Trust (2015) 'National Trust launches ambitious plan to nurse natural environment back to health', press release, March. Available at: www.nationaltrust.org.uk

[13] *Farmers' Guardian* (2015) 'National Trust blasted for attack on unsustainable farming', 27 March. Available at: www.fginsight.com

[14] Hovesen, P., interviewed January 2015.

[15] Truss, L. (2014) 'Speech at Northern Farming Conference', November. Available at: www.defra.gov.uk

[16] Truss, L. (2015) 'Speech at Oxford Farming Conference', January. Available at: www.ofc.org.uk/archive/2015

[17] See: www.farmingdelivers.co.uk

[18] NFU (2015) 'Backing British farming in a volatile world'. Available at: www.nfuonline.com/635-15tl-the-report-digital-low-res/

[19] Soil Association (2015) press release, 24 February. Available at: press@soilassociation.org

[20] Hovesen, P., interviewed January 2015, Holkham Estate.

[21] *Financial Times* (2015) 'UK farm land returns more than Mayfair', 18 February.

[22] Beedell, J. interviewed November 2014.

[23] Moulds, J. and Treanor, J. (2014) 'Co-op sells farms business to Wellcome Trust', *The Guardian*, 4 August.

[24] See: www.greenshieldsagri.com

[25] Dunn, G., interviewed February 2015 .

[26] Oxford Farming Conference, 7 January 2015, Session 1 – Politics. Available at: ofc.org.uk

FOUR

Land secure?

You forget that the fruits belong to all and that the land belongs to no one.[1]

How do you measure the influence of the aristocracy? Northumberland, ultimate county of the landed class and fiefdom of the Percys, is a good place to start. For centuries, Alnwick Castle, a magnificent medieval stronghold set in rolling parkland beside an agreeable market town, has been the seat of power for a family that traces its roots to a William di Percy. He came to England with William the Conqueror in 1066. Whether the castle remains so powerful today is a matter of debate. However, what cannot be disputed is the influence of the inhabitants – albeit, now exercised discreetly – since a successor, Henry Percy, acquired the border fortress, and its surrounding lands, from the Bishop of Durham in 1309.

The role of the family enterprise, Northumberland Estates, in the economy of the county and in its social and political networks cannot be underestimated. Like other old, landed undertakings, it has morphed into a powerful development enterprise, exploiting its key asset – land and attendant buildings – to the maximum. For better or for worse, it is a powerful player in the county – accepted by some, tolerated by others, if not universally popular, and boasting 'an international property portfolio centred on the north east'.[2] This includes 'stunning mansion houses' – Alnwick Castle, as well as Syon House, in West London, for starters – as well as numerous other properties, over 100,000 farming acres either directly managed by the estate or let to 100 tenant farmers, mineral rights over 300,000 acres, 800 cottages, countless farm buildings and 'valuable development land around Tyneside'.

Next to Windsor, a home of the Royals, Alnwick is the country's second-largest inhabited castle. It has a firm place in history: Harry Hotspur, immortalised in Shakespeare's *Henry IV, Part 1*, was the son of the fourth Lord Percy. In its present form, the stronghold dates back to 1752. Sir Hugh Percy, the first duke after a succession of earls, turned a rundown military structure into today's mix of old castle, traditional stately home and – let us not mince words – small palace, complete with Italianate staterooms and one of the 'finest collections of renaissance art in Europe', according to its website. In 2004, to raise some cash, the Duke sold Raphael's *The Madonna of the Pinks* to the National Gallery for £22 million; in 2014, he raised a further £30 million by selling a wide range of art – including work by the Flemish artist Jan Brueghel – in order to meet a huge repair bill for flood damage to a housing development at Newcastle upon Tyne after a culvert collapsed on land owned by Northumberland Estates.

Today, the incumbent, Ralph George Algernon Percy, the 12th Duke of Northumberland, might appear a shadow of his predecessors – cautious in the limelight while his wife is clearly more comfortable in it. Jane Percy, Duchess of Northumberland, is the county's Lord Lieutenant, the Queen's representative. She features more prominently in the local media than many politicians. The Windsors and the Percys are friends, albeit that the lands of the former – directly and indirectly – outnumber those of the latter. Theirs is a familiar relationship in aristocratic society, where the bonds between the landed class and royalty remain strong; the Queen, after all, has substantial personal estates at Balmoral, on Deeside in Scotland, and at Sandringham in North Norfolk.

Alnwick Castle: a majestic stronghold, in a county dominated by big landowners, and seat of the Percys since 1309. (Source: Andrew Farrell)

Meeting the Duke across the kitchen table of the family quarters in Alnwick Castle provides an insight into the philosophy of the family firm, which has its detractors in the North-East.[3] He is both agreeably candid and forthcoming about the challenges facing a landed dynasty. Perhaps with a touch of self-deprecation, he even volunteers – quite seriously, I think – that a committee, rather than the current owners, could probably run the enterprise.

"A committee? Really?", I ask. He replies:

> "From a financial point of view, maybe. I think you do need personal direction, as long as they haven't gone raving mad ... and, perhaps, a family that's been here for 700 years might have a bit of experience in that department."

But how does he justify this longevity of ownership?

"I often think about it. It is difficult for me to answer that. Once I've passed away, people can say 'Well, perhaps he did a good job or he did a hopeless job' … but I have tried to run the estate in a balanced way, protect the heritage obviously, which is the principal concern of the estate, without damaging the landscape too much … of course there are compromises, there are times when you need to raise capital and become unpopular with locals when you are trying to do developments of one sort or the other, but that's all part of the balance of estate management."

Eight years after succeeding to the dukedom in 1995, after the death of Henry, his older brother, Ralph Percy signalled a more commercial ethos in the family firm. This approach seems to have continued apace. He is a professional land surveyor schooled in estate management, who gained considerable experience turning round the finances, and the structure, of the family's smaller 3,000-acre Albury estate in Surrey. Since the succession, the turnaround in the larger estate's fortunes in Northumberland has been significant. In 1995, for instance, 48% of the rental income of Northumberland Estates came from agriculture; 20 years later, this has dropped to 18%. Commercial development (67%) has taken up much of the slack.

The Duke hands me a small book he has written, lavishly illustrated with photographs of the Percy lands, property, heirlooms, staff and extensive art collection. It includes one overriding message: 'The estate may seem rooted in the past, but it is constantly changing in order to survive.'[4] This has meant raising capital from exploiting the development potential of land, including chunks of industrial Tyneside, for housing, leisure and commercial and industrial building. As he acknowledged – and as headlines in the local press attest – it can make Northumberland Estates unpopular. As a Liberal Democrat general election candidate noted early in January 2015: 'Northumberland Estates own a huge amount of development land in and around many of our towns and villages and, as a result, hold a great deal of power over the future of communities.'[5]

I suggest that when either an individual or a family trust owns such a large slice of a county, it can often seem like a de facto planning authority in its own right, relatively unchallengeable: "If you look historically, we played a huge part in providing schooling, churches, hospitals – all sorts – in our area of influence", the Duke replies:

> "In the days when coal provided big revenues (as it once did for several big landowners), it was a pretty powerful estate. It did dominate the area, rather less so now. I would like to think that democracy has curbed us."

In 2002, a group of rural academics described the Duke's outlook as more akin to that of a "property developer" – with a caveat. His enterprise prefers to retain ownership of its diversified assets, such as business and retail parks, on – say – 99-year leases in order to enhance long-term income flows.[6] When, occasionally, small amounts of development land are sold, the estate "usually ploughs back most of the capital into buying more land; typically a small farm close to a village with development potential."

Although rooted in history, the Percy empire - which also embraces a large mansion (Syon House) and surrounding small estate in west London and a 12,000-acre estate in the Scottish Borders – is evolving and adapting to a modern property market. It is an approach adopted by other – but by no means all – landed dynasties.

To be fair, the old landed class are a diverse bunch – sometimes paternalistic, sometimes aggressively commercial, invariably business-focused – and they are sometimes, from my experience, more accessible than large institutions, which might be termed either semi-state-cum-semi-royal or charitable. These institutions exercise considerable power.

Take the Crown Estate, often incorrectly seen as the Queen's direct personal fiefdom, which can trace its roots back to 1066 when all land belonged to the monarch 'in right of the Crown'. By 1760, George III agreed that he would accept a stipend from Parliament – the Civil List – and, in return, surrendered the revenues from the Crown Estate. When Victoria took the throne in 1841, it had 106,000 acres; by 1890, it had over 220,000. Today, it has around 360,000 acres of rural land plus forests, residential and commercial property, extensive mineral rights, marinas, ports, and harbours.

In fact, although the Queen officially 'holds' the estate, all its profits – over £2.2 billion over the last 10 years – go to the Treasury. It is a semi-state body, run by an independent board, which is not allowed to borrow and yet prides itself as being 'an independent commercial business' – or, as an official put it to me, an "income-driven total return business".

The Royals, at the very least, are kept informed. Alison Nimmo, the Crown Estate's chief executive, gives the Queen an annual update and sees the Prince of Wales every six months.[7] Revealingly, she added in April 2015: "Obviously, we have a close day-to-day relationship, but they leave us to get on with the business. They seem very happy with what we're doing."

It is a considerable operation. Aside from those 360,000 acres, it manages 15,800 acres of the Windsor estate and owns London's Regent Street and much of the adjoining St James, half of the UK's shoreline, and the UK seabed out to 12 nautical miles, for instance. Multimillion pound annual revenues from the Crown Estate's interests in Scotland – four estates, including Glenlivet on Speyside, salmon fishing rights and much else – will shortly be transferred from the Treasury to the Scottish Parliament.

As Cahill[8] has noted, the Crown Estate and the Duchy of Cornwall (created by Edward III in 1337) – whose 140,000 acres, largely in South-West England, provide an income for the Prince of Wales – are the largest related land holdings in the country, 'which between them constitute the largest two agricultural conglomerates in the UK'. He has said that unless Parliament calls a halt to what amounts to 'state purchases for a private endowment', these two holdings will achieve near-monopolistic status in the real estate market.

When the Crown Estate bought the 4,500-acre Ellington Estate in Northumberland for a reported £20 million from the metals and mining giant Rio Tinto in 2014, Ken Jones, its rural and coastal portfolio director, underlined its commercial approach: "As with all the assets in our portfolio, we are keen to drive best value from the estate."[9] That, he said, included the possibility of housing. Of course, different estates – whether private, publicly owned or charitable – have widely divergent management philosophies, from the uncompromisingly commercial, sweating assets to the maximum, to the more benign and pragmatic.

Over the years, I have interviewed a range of aristocrats out of a fascination with a way of life seemingly detached from the world occupied by the vast majority and rooted in another age of deference. They range from the richest of all (the Duke of Westminster) to the landowner with by far the largest private estate (the Duke of Buccleuch and Queensberry) and a third running one of Britain's most productive farming operations (Thomas Coke, Earl of Leicester). It has been a

The Duke of Buccleuch and Queensberry (pictured outside Drumlanrig Castle) heads Britain's biggest private landowning concern. He laments that the inter-war years brought an "era of ultimately penal taxation that put paid to many old families and their traditional lands". Now he fears Scottish land reform will further cut the size of his estates.
Source: Buccleuch Estates

fascinating journey, confirming some views, moderating others – but never dull.

If we are honest, our views on the aristocracy are both complex and contradictory. As the French economist Thomas Piketty[10] notes, wealth has become so concentrated in advanced economies that most people are unaware of its existence: in the case of the old aristocracy, it can be hidden in a labyrinth of trusts and other 'tax-efficient' vehicles – sometimes, even unregistered with the Land Registry (see Chapter Five) – behind the high walls of some estates.

While we are awestruck by the great houses of the old landed class – none greater than Coke's magnificent 18th-century Palladian pile at Holkham, North Norfolk – we should certainly question their continued dominance of some counties. Furthermore, it is certainly reasonable to ask whether this inherited dominance serves both the country and the countryside well. Put simply, are the aristocracy using their land and inherited wealth to benefit us all, rather than a select few in the family firm?

In Scotland, as we shall see, the Scottish National Party (SNP) government is providing one answer: namely, in some cases, they are serving the country badly. Consequently, the break-up of some large Scottish estates is now seen as inevitable – by the landowners themselves. In a revealing interview, Richard Scott, the Duke of Buccleuch and Queensberry – also a significant landowner in England, with 11,000 acres at Boughton in Northamptonshire – made clear his frustration and anger. In near-apocalyptic tones, he spoke of a "pivotal moment" being reached with the prospect of his three large Scottish estates shrinking by a quarter – or by well over 50,000 acres: "What is the point of hanging on to it all and being shot at by the Left for your pains?", he asked plaintively.[11]

His cousin, Ralph Percy, Duke of Northumberland – conversely, a Scottish landowner, too – tried to put ownership and the public good into a wider perspective:

> "If you were sensible about land … you would think here's a guy, or trustees [family trusts legally own most large estates], they own

all this land, they're investing in it the whole time, they look after it – maintain all the roads, the tracks, the infrastructure – and the great British public enjoy it, they have it, they can walk almost everywhere, and we look after it. If you bring in land reform, and nationalise it – whatever – someone else has to pay for it."[12]

Of course, the maintenance of big estates, and their grand houses and castles, does not come cheap; upkeep of Alnwick Castle alone now costs £1.5 million annually, with another £1 million spent on what the Duke calls "other heritage properties…. Grade 2 listed properties all over the place", while Alnwick's splendid parks have 12 miles of walls to maintain. What is more, he says, Syon House in West London is "not in great nick".

Putting that to one side, can our preconceptions of a rich, landowning class out of touch with both larger society and with reality – here, I hold my hand up – be over-simplified? Much as we might instinctively rail against inherited wealth, and its perceived evils, will an enforced break-up of estates necessarily lead to the progressive outcome we might desire – namely, better use of land, more efficient agriculture and an easier path for young people into farming? In truth, some landowners, such as the Cokes – pioneers of crop rotation to improve soil quality on their 26,000-acre Holkham Estate in North Norfolk – run efficient farming operations recognised not only as progressive and sustainable, but also as setting a benchmark for the rest.

Others, of course, fall short of this objective. They can be insular, self-interested, detached and – yes – arrogant in the assumption that what is beneficial for the family firm must be good for the area in which they operate. A high public profile, regardless of ownership, does not necessarily match a progressive approach to landlord–tenant relations, as the National Trust underlines.

The National Trust is one of the largest landowners, with 630,000 acres, far outstripping any private concern or landed family trust. With over 1,500 farming tenants and a further 5,000 housing tenants, it might be viewed by its 4.2 million members as a benign landlord in keeping with an overarching mantra: 'For places, for ever, for everyone.' Yet, with echoes of yesteryear – of a seemingly distant, uncaring landlord – it has, as outlined in Chapter Three, been mired in a dispute with tenants, leaving some feeling threatened.

In short, generalisations between private landlords and their counterparts in the charitable and public sectors are best avoided. For instance, interviewing the late Duke of Buccleuch[13] in 1999 at an event marking the publication of the Scottish government's first land reform proposals, he acknowledged the shortcomings of some big estates: "If there are a few bad apples in the basket, let's get rid of them", he railed. He then made this point directly to the late Scottish First Minister Donald Dewar: "Does he agree that blanket accusations of landowners abusing their powers relate to a small handful out of thousands?" As we shall see, it is a question still being hotly debated north of the border, but not in England – yet.

The foundations for the successful landowning dynasty, at Holkham, were laid in the 16th century by Sir Edward Coke, variously speaker of the House of Commons and attorney general to both Elizabeth I and King James. His successors built one of England's finest country houses, Holkham Hall, hub of a family enterprise embracing tourism, farming and property. It is headed by the Earl of Leicester, Thomas Edward Coke – pronounced 'Cook' – whose business employs 200 full-time staff, including six gamekeepers, a conservation manager, an education officer and one butler.

In his office, overlooking splendid parkland and herds of grazing deer among broad oaks, he recounts how the estate – beset by "prohibitive" death duties between the wars, and a wage bill including 50 servants – almost passed to the National Trust in the late 1940s. It was, he reflects, "our Downton Abbey moment".[14] Whether it would have remained the efficient farming operation it is today if the ownership had passed to the Trust is an open question. Fortunately, the Earl's grandfather vetoed the Trust takeover and his late father, the 7th Earl of Leicester, put Holkham on a sounder business footing after it had incurred big losses. Today, it is a thriving enterprise of separate businesses.

But how can the landed class justify their inheritance and good fortune? Thomas Coke, who lives in part of the hall with his wife,

Polly, and four children, is disarmingly honest: "I used to say I was met with guilt – 'How come this is all mine?'", he responds candidly; "But it is a huge responsibility. We are very public spirited ... do a lot for the community. If I did not have this responsibility I could sit at home and read a book."

I put a similar question to Richard Scott, the current Duke of Buccleuch and Queensberry, by far Britain's biggest private landowner, with around 240,000 acres, mainly in Scotland. How did he react when people complained about the aristocracy 'having it easy, inheriting all this wealth and land, all these country houses, sitting pretty'? "We are incredibly fortunate and privileged", he replied calmly in the splendid library of Bowhill, one of his homes near Selkirk in the Scottish Borders:

> "I am certainly not going to imply ... we are sitting here with a white man's burden. That's a dreadful image to portray. I think there are huge pleasures from this wonderful rich and varied inheritance we have but it has its complications and its frustrations."

Richard Scott's cousin, Ralph Percy, Duke of Northumberland, was equally forthcoming:

> "I do remember when my brother died [in 1995] thinking 'My God, our lives are going to change dramatically'. We had rather a nice family farm house in North Northumberland and we were suddenly thrown into something I certainly was not ready for ... but I am not complaining. There are huge privileges with it as well. I don't have a bad life on the whole."

But one estate empire stands supreme. The Duke of Westminster, Gerald Cavendish Grosvenor, one of Britain's richest men, has a property portfolio at home and overseas that, in value, dwarfs every landed estate. With his Grosvenor Group shares owned by family trusts, private assets include 165,000 acres of rural land, a dairy farm,

The Duke of Northumberland in the extensive parkland overlooking the Cheviot Hills near Alnwick Castle

the UK's largest bull stud and the Chester Grosvenor Hotel near the family seat, Eaton Hall in Cheshire. Alongside this – the really big cash cow – is the Grosvenor Group's freehold of 300 acres in London's Mayfair and Belgravia, plus large chunks of Park Lane – truly, some of the most valuable land in the world.[15]

When I interviewed the Duke of Westminster at Eaton Hall, he saw no reason to justify what he called the "longevity of ownership" – provided a landowner stays in Britain, provides work and wealth, and forgoes the pleasures of a carefree life in the sun:

"[Wealth?] I am not in the business of justifying it. I am using it to create more money and more jobs. We take pride in the fact that we employ more people than in Victorian times ... inherited wealth is only justified if it is perceived to be used in a responsible manner ... it can't be if the present-day beneficiary tears off and squanders it … sits back sunning himself in Monte Carlo saying 'To hell with the world.'"[16]

The survival – sometimes the expansion – of these aristocratic empires is a story of resilience, power play and, latterly, transformation into commercial property and development enterprises beyond the traditional farming estate and a string of agricultural tenancies – once the bedrock of these family firms. Theirs is a society, paradoxically, apart from the Britain most of us inhabit, yet still a powerful part of some local and regional economies: developing land for commercial and residential use, for instance, or, maybe, blocking proposals that do not fit a perceived narrow interest. As one academic study of Northumberland has noted, a long-standing and traditional economic institution – the estate – has thus become 'entwined within local development networks in terms of planning and economic development'.[17]

As a once-dominant ruling class, Britain's aristocracy has recovered from a 17th-century insurrection (although landowners in the English Civil War were divided between Royalists and Parliamentarians), a political onslaught from a radical Liberal prime minister in the early 20th century, seemingly oppressive taxation subsequently and a relatively peaceful transfer of landownership from tenancies to owner-occupation between two world wars leading to a break-up of many large holdings. It has also seen off Labour's threat of land nationalisation after 1945. That the aristocracy has survived, and often prospered, after a period of severe contraction – albeit, sometimes morphing into private development companies – is a testament not only to its endurance, but also to its deep establishment roots.

Set against Britain barely 150 years ago, this is no mean feat. Then, all land was owned by less than 5% of Britain's population. The aristocracy, and its best friend – the monarchy – reigned supreme. Conventions asserting collective rights over common land had been extinguished through the Enclosures. Most people owned little of substance.

Now, approaching 70% of the population – the property-owning class – have a stake in land, however small. However, their modest semis, terraces and small detached piles take up a tiny space of our 60 million acres. The largest number of landowners, in short, collectively own the smallest pieces of land.

Remarkably, the landed aristocracy alongside the new rich, government agencies (such as the Forestry Commission and Defence Estates) and that powerful semi-state institution, the Crown Estate, remain powerful players: consolidating holdings, buying land, trading it and developing elsewhere on urban fringes and in city centres, for instance.

Overall, perhaps a third of our land is still in the hands of the aristocracy. As Hugh Ellis and Kate Henderson note, this equates to a group of just 36,000 people – 0.6% of the population – owning half the rural land in England alone.[18]

In Northumberland, little has changed to alter the balance of landownership since the publication of an extensive national survey in the 1870s. Known officially as *The return of owners of land* – unofficially as the 'New Domesday' – it found that half of the county was owned by the landed aristocracy. This was higher than in any other English county aside from tiny Rutland.

In 2002, Newcastle University academics found that large estates still covered half the county of Northumberland.[19] The largest of all comprised those 100,000-plus acres belonging to the Duke of Northumberland, alongside mineral rights over more than 300,000 acres. For the time being, his family firm is still sitting relatively pretty after 700 years. Ditto his counterparts elsewhere in England – but not, significantly, in Scotland.

Notes

[1] Rousseau, J.-J. (1913 [1761]) *The social contract and the discourses,* London: J.M. Dent and Sons Ltd.

[2] See: www.northumberlandestates.co.uk

[3] Percy, R., Duke of Northumberland, interviewed May 2015, at Alnwick Castle.

[4] Percy, R., *Northumberland Estates: The management of a great landed estate*, Derby: Heritage House Group.

[5] *The Journal* (2015) 'Duke under fire over homes plan', 23 January. Available at: www.thejournal.co.uk

[6] Murdoch, J., Lowe, P., Ward, N. and Marsden, P. (2002) *The differentiated countryside*, London: Routledge.

[7] Shah, O. (2015) 'By royal appointment, I spend my days playing monopoly for real', *Sunday Times,* 5 April. Available at: www.thesundaytimes.co.uk

[8] Cahill, K. (2001) *Who owns Britain*, Edinburgh: Canongate, p 74.

[9] Lognonne, R. (2014) 'Crown Estate buys Alcan site – sale prompts fears of spoiled landscape in Northumberland', *The Journal*, 24 February. Available at: www.thejournal.co.uk

[10] Piketty, T. (2014) *Capital in the twenty-first century*, Harvard University Press.

[11] Scott, R., the Duke of Buccleuch and Queensberry, interviewed at Bowhill, Scottish Borders, October 2014.

[12] Percy, R., Duke of Northumberland, interviewed May 2015, at Alnwick Castle.

[13] Hetherington, P. (1999) 'Laird of 250,000 acres warns of false utopias', *The Guardian*, 6 January.

[14] Coke, T., Earl of Leicester, interviewed January 2015, at Holkham Hall, Norfolk.

[15] *Sunday Times Rich List* (2015) 'Duke still growing his family fortune', April 26, p 22.

[16] Hetherington, P. (1993) 'Kind hearts and coronet', *The Guardian,* 27 September.

[17] Murdoch, J., Lowe, P., Ward, N. and Marsden, P. (2002) *The differentiated countryside*, London: Routledge, p 119.

[18] Ellis, H. and Henderson, K. (2014) *Rebuilding Britain: planning for a better future*, Bristol: Policy Press.

[19] Murdoch, J., Lowe, P., Ward, N. and Marsden, P. (2002) *The differentiated countryside*, London: Routledge.

FIVE

Unclear ownership

This is the judgement of sober men
Will be this long desired Registry
Upon whose fond none can be cheated when
They trade and trust on that security.[1]

To gain a full picture of our land – use, abuse, underused potential and, increasingly, exposure to flooding and climate change – it is clearly essential to know who owns what. That means all of it, and not simply selective chunks of Britain held by the state in various forms alongside large charities, such as the National Trust, speculators and private landowners.

Early in the life of the 2010–15 Conservative-led government, a senior director of the Royal Institution of Chartered Surveyors – who has considerable experience working abroad – made the point to me graphically: 'If we do not know what we've got how can we manage it?', he asked rhetorically; 'This is a national resource and we need to know – quite an irony when you think about it for a country ... which is the best mapped in the world through the Ordnance Survey.'[2] It is a reasonable question.

Ninety years after a state agency, the Land Registry, was given the legislative teeth to detail the ownership of all land in England and Wales, officially 15% of our land remains 'unregistered'. Full registration was scheduled for 2011. Now, a time limit has been abandoned. To try to be fair, over the last four years, a push has apparently been under way: for instance, the Forestry Commission (with 2.5 million acres), Defence Estates and the Crown Estate have signed up voluntarily, according to the Land Registry. However, the Land Registry cautiously adds that "We do not know whether this is all of their land holdings as we only register what they lodge."[3]

One problem is that so much of our land, often owned by the old aristocracy, has never officially changed hands since registration was introduced again in 1925. Hence, it has not been logged because a sale, in official jargon, marks a 'trigger point' for recording transactions. Another is that various devices have been used to keep land 'in the family', even if it has, technically, changed hands; and a third problem is that there is no compulsion to register anyway.

A fourth problem involves the limited scope of registration, according to Richard Munton, emeritus Professor of Geography at University College London (UCL), a leading rural academic.[4] He was an adviser to the Northfield Committee, the last major government-commissioned inquiry into land use in the UK. Its 1979 report into the Acquisition and Occupancy of Agricultural Land – a response to growing concerns about big institutions buying farm land – found flaws in the scope of the registration process because it logged 'legal' title rather than 'beneficial' ownership. In other words, tax avoidance has apparently encouraged the creation of family partnerships, trusts or even 'fiscal tenancies' that distance such ownership from managerial control. Munton also complains that the land registration system has little to offer in defining land use – crucial, you might think, if we are to have a rational debate about the utilisation, and the abuse, of our most basic resource.

Taking up this point, Kevin Cahill,[5] the writer and campaigner who undertook the most detailed recent study of British landownership in 2002, has noted that failure to record all titles does not arise from the

Wind turbines on the Ellington Estate, bought last year for a reported £20m by the Crown Estate to add to its 360,000-acre rural land portfolio – and, hence, logged by the Land Registry. But elsewhere in Britain much land still remains unregistered.

actions of the Land Registry. Rather, says Cahill, failure comes from the way it was constructed 'by lawyers on behalf of landowners [and] designed to conceal ownership, not reveal it'. Why?

Some have already speculated that voluntary, rather than compulsory, registration was driven by a fear that a future government might consider a comprehensive system of land taxation and, ultimately, nationalisation of all land; the Land Registry, after all, was ostensibly given more legislative powers in 1925 at a time when ownership was a burning political issue and large estates – as already noted – were being broken up for a variety of reasons. Whatever the reasoning behind a voluntary system, Cahill – who lives in Exeter – remains sceptical that registration has even reached 85%: "I find that hard to believe ... most of the landowners I know have refused [to register]", he maintains; "They could not see the point."

Amid today's land trading, another question arises: the operation of an opaque, 'shadow' market, yet to be quantified, in which housing developers take legal options to buy land at a later date in order to reduce their risk before planning permission is granted.[6] There is no official record of the scale of this (unregistered) activity – of which more in Chapter Six – although tens of thousands of acres could be tied up.

The Land Registry itself has moved from the Georgian splendour of Lincoln's Inn Fields, the country's pre-eminent legal quarter in Central London, to the outer reaches of the capital and an anonymous office block in nondescript Croydon. In an oak-panelled suite, incongruously transplanted from Lincoln's Inn and fitted out for another age, Mike Westcott-Rudd, the Land Registry's head of corporate legal services, explains their limitations: "We cannot force them [landowners] to register ... there is no law that says you can."[7] He cautions that any compulsion could violate the European Convention of Human Rights, that some estates have been in the same family for nigh-on 1,000 years and that various devices have been used to ensure that titles do not change when estates are vested by fathers – usually before they die – to eldest sons: "Property can therefore be passed from father to son without the transfer of a legal estate, which would trigger first registration", he explains.

In reality, the task of full registration should not be onerous. The Romans, after all, made a good attempt at it with regular censuses, which formed the basis of a land tax. Similarly, the Anglo Saxons subsequently levied a land tax – *Danegeld* – which would have required details of landownership. Their initiative culminated in the remarkable Domesday Book in 1086, which recorded all landowners. It was a survey undertaken with such care that the Land Registry itself records, in its own history, that William the Conqueror knew of every 'hide of land in England ... who held it and how much it was worth'.[8] Significantly, the Registry acknowledged in this history that 'the [original] Domesday Book was just about the last land register in this country for taxation purposes'. That was 929 years ago.

Matters then drifted for centuries. Finally, an attempt was made at charting ownership at the end of the 18th century by creating a Board of Agriculture. The aim was to improve production on farms – the first stab, according to Peter Clery, to 'find out what was actually going on in rural England'.[9]

This, it seemed, proved successful: the cultivated area of England had increased by a fifth to 2 million acres, and by the early 19th century, the Cokes' estate, at Holkham in Norfolk, became an international attraction for farmers keen to discover new farming practices combining grazing with crop rotation from as far afield as the US and Russia. By 1816, the Board of Agriculture, fired with a new activism, undertook another survey to discover the causes of an unexpected agricultural depression, which saw thousands of rural workers leave for the Americas in search of a new life.

A subsequent, more serious, attempt came towards the end of the 19th century, partly to answer – and stem – a growing campaign for land reform and to address the concerns of those who railed against a small number of aristocrats owning a large slice of Britain. It was labelled the 'Second', 'Little' or 'New' Domesday Book – officially known as *The return of owners of land* – and it was published in four volumes between 1874 and 1876. For Cahill it is 'our lost book, a social, historical and present treasure that academic and social historians have largely ignored'. It is relevant today, he says, because – in the absence of full registration – it provides the only way to trace the ownership of considerable acreages of land in England and Wales.[10]

Consider this: almost all houses – the main assets of a majority of people – have been recorded since legislation in 1925 required any land transaction in England and Wales to be registered. However, a large number of estates mentioned in the 'Second' Domesday Book – they include Oxbridge colleges, endowed with considerable land – have made no official transactions since then. If they have sold off land, the core of their estates have remained intact and 'un-transacted'.

As Cahill has noted, after publication of the 1876 'Second Domesday Book' anyone could buy its four volumes for the equivalent of £128, but under the 1925 Act, he says, 'a steel shutter came down'. As a result, all the large estates identified in 1876 were 'sent back into medieval obscurity in 1925 [and] many remain there still … the largest landowners … remain, in many cases unrecorded.'[11] Thus, as democracy advanced, information retreated.

Before 1925, it seemed, matters were more transparent. In Peter Clery's[12] words, the 'Second Domesday', meant to counter claims of a concentration of ownership, proved the opposite, namely, by revealing 'a colossal concentration of land in very few hands', with 363 families alone owning a quarter of England. Cahill says that it exposed the iniquity of ownership in Victorian Britain, with all land in the UK 'owned' by just 4.5% of the population, while 95.5% owned nothing.[13] A very small aristocratic network, most of whom had dual links with the two Houses of Parliament, thus controlled almost everything.

Above all, the Second Domesday Book proved remarkable in another respect: given the interminable time being taken to complete the present registration process, it recorded the ownership of 98% of all land in England, Scotland, Wales and (pre-partition) Ireland in just four years. However, Mike Westcott-Rudd, of the Land Registry, says comparisons between the Second Domesday Book and the current registration process are misleading because, he insists, the former was a compulsory step towards a land tax and was imprecise. The current drive, he maintains, is more precise, with each property based on Ordnance Survey mapping. However, it fails to answer an all-important question: how much land is suitable, or available, for farming and for housing – and from whom might it be obtained?

Notes

[1] Yarranton, A. (2000) 'A plain dealer's prayer for a registry', in Mayer, P. and Pemberton, A., *A short history of land registration in England and Wales*, Land Registry.

[2] Hetherington, P. (2011) 'Whose land it is anyway?', *Modus*, monthly magazine of the Royal Institution of Chartered Surveyors, May.

[3] Westcott-Rudd, M., interviewed November 2014, at Land Registry, Croydon.

[4] Munton, R., 'Rural land ownership in the UK: changing patterns and future possibilities for land use policy'. Available at: www.elsevier.com/locate/landusepol

[5] Cahill, K. (2011) The great property swindle, *New Statesman*, 7 March.

[6] Lyons, M., 'The Lyons housing review', report of independent housing commission established by former Labour leader Ed Miliband. Available at: www.yourbritain.org.uk/uploads/editor/files/The_Lyons_Housing_Review_2.pdf, p 62.

[7] Westcott-Rudd, M., interviewed November 2014.

[8] Mayer, P. and Pemberton, A. (2000) *A short history of land registration in England and Wales*, Land Registry, p 3.

[9] Clery, P. (2012) *Green gold: a thousand years of English land*, Phillimore, p 57.

[10] Cahill, K. (2011) 'The great property swindle', *New Statesman*, 7 March.

[11] Cahill, K. (2012) Essay for seminar, House of Lords, Committee room G, 4 December 2012.

[12] Clery, P. (2012) *Green gold: a thousand years of English land*, Phillimore.

[13] Cahill, K. (2011) 'The great property swindle', *New Statesman*, 7 March.

SIX

Land for the people

This is the true nature of home – it is a place of peace; the shelter.[1]

Three months before the 2015 general election, a Conservative councillor in South Lincolnshire, exasperated by the rocketing price of development land, threw political caution to the wind. Challenging the laissez-faire approach of his party, Roger Gambba-Jones called for measures to curb land speculation. Such action, he thought, was one way of making housing more affordable.

In a letter to the bimonthly journal of the Local Government Association, he railed: 'The major cause of our housing quality crisis is the price of land. The owner of a field can increase its agricultural value by a hundred fold [if he sells] for commercial development and two hundred times for residential.'[2] Little wonder, then, that despite allocating sites for housing in a local plan, authorities like his own – South Holland District Council – were powerless when potential building land remained undeveloped: 'It might bring horror to many Conservatives, I know, but unless we get to grips with this we won't be able to house people properly', he explained later.

Gambba-Jones is living proof that the case for land reform transcends political allegiance. To say that forcing more transparency in land trading and clamping down on speculation – perhaps by ending inheritance tax relief and other generous fiscal concessions – somehow interferes with the market economy (as some on the political Right claim) misses the point. Agriculture, after all, is the last great subsidised industry, operating outside the norms of a free market. It gets at least £2 billion annually in a generous 'rural payment' regime from taxpayers through the European Union's (EU's) Common Agricultural Policy. Regardless of the state of the national economy and the efficiency, or the prosperity, of farmers – be they 'barley barons' in Eastern England, the Prince of Wales, tenants on his vast Duchy of Cornwall estate or an upland farmer in the North Pennines – the subsidy cheques keep rolling in.

To take Gambba-Jones' argument to its logical conclusion, are we paying farmers and landowners handsomely to keep land off the market, notably, around urban fringes? If that is the case, our most basic resource – our land – is being rationed in the face of a housing crisis, with owners expecting a windfall as land prices rocket further into the valuation stratosphere. This uplift in value from planning permission encourages a high level of land trading, rather than development, eventually resulting in windfalls for the landowner rather than the local community. With competition fierce in this opaque, unregulated market, and no official data outlining the scale of trading, one casualty is the quality and the size of homes: they are getting smaller. The other casualty is the small building concern, squeezed out by high land prices: they are becoming fewer. Around three quarters of new homes are now built by a small group of volume builders.[3]

Late in 2014, the Lyons Housing Review Commission[4] – whose wide membership embraced the housing, development and planning sectors – warned that an artificial scarcity of land was distorting the housing market, limiting building and 'incentivising the acquisition and trading of land'. The Commission spoke of six firms of land agents alone holding strategic land banks of 23,000 acres – enough for up to 400,000 homes at current building densities. It expressed particular concern that 'non-developers' – farmers, landowners, institutions – were holding on to land either under an option (for developers) or with planning permission. Although they had no intention of currently building, according to Lyons, they 'may be motivated by speculating on future land values'.

'Options' are a familiar tool in the arcane development world. They involve a legal agreement in which a volume builder reserves land from an owner and buys at a later date, usually a fixed period. This means that large chunks of our land suitable for housing are tied up in secret deals. Crucially, this land is not available to others who might want to build more immediately. Some have labelled the practice a 'shadow market' driven by builders and developers, particularly on the country's urban fringes.[5] Cynically, you might call this a risk-free way of bolstering a balance sheet through an expanded 'land bank' owned by someone else – without the need for an immediate sale.

Clearly, we need to know the scale of this activity if we are to begin to address the pressing need for more housing on our land. Perhaps this could be achieved by making it a legal requirement to register land option agreements – thus bringing transparency to this unquantifiable 'shadow' market. As discussed in Chapter Five, Lyons' recommendation to give the Land Registry the task of opening up information on landownership for public scrutiny – in a similar way to property price transactions – at least deserves consideration.

Such a step would go down well in South Lincolnshire. When he moved to Spalding in 1996, Gambba-Jones says he saw agricultural land trading at around £1,000 an acre. Now, he says it can be going for at least 20 times more, fuelled by overseas buyers – some doubtless with an eye on a longer-term windfall from potential development land – and readily available borrowing from banks. Seemingly untroubled by their lending excesses, which triggered the 2007/08 global financial meltdown, banks see land as a safe bet – for now, anyway.

Lincolnshire highlights the twin pressures facing our land. It not only offers some of Britain's best crop-growing acres, as the billionaire industrialist James Dyson can attest (see Chapter Three). In the south of the county, it is also seen as ripe for development, effectively an appendage of nearby Peterborough with a rail-hub offering quick access to both London and booming Cambridge.

Spalding is, thus, getting new housing estates, with small identikit homes, 'Noddy boxes' in the vernacular of our times. 'Developers … pay a premium and then build to the lowest possible standards', laments Gambba-Jones. Even worse, he says, the last government – 'instead of dealing with the land price issue' – latterly removed any social obligation for developers to provide affordable housing on sites in places like Lincolnshire, where incomes are low.

To label England's housing model dysfunctional is an understatement. It is broken. Bluntly, the use and abuse of our land takes no account of the nation's needs. In England alone, where the shortage is most acute, we should be building 245,000 homes annually to address rising household formation. The figure has not even reached half that level since the 2010 election. In 2014, 118,760 homes were completed.[6] And the number of homes started in the same period – 137,000 – was hailed as a great success by the Home Builders Federation.[7]

This falls well short of addressing the shortage because we are failing to deal with the real problem, namely, an effective withdrawal of the state from funding social and affordable homes. If history tells us anything, it is that building homes, for all incomes and tenures, can only be ramped up with substantial state investment – initially, anyway. As we shall see, if governments take the long view, much of that investment can be repaid.

But where to build? The debate, in truth, is full of contradictions. It centres on whether more homes can be accommodated on 'brownfield', or previously developed, land, without the need for a substantial number, if any at all, on 'greenfield' sites – not to be confused with the 'green belt', a quite separate concept, circling big conurbations such as Greater London, where building is generally prohibited in order to avoid urban sprawl.

This has led to a perverse outcome: while housing is generally seen as desirable – for we all want a decent home, after all, for ourselves and for our children – development is paradoxically viewed as a threat. Opinion polling underlines the success of the self-styled 'countryside lobby' in peddling the myth that our land is overcrowded: almost two thirds of respondents in one survey, for instance, thought that between a quarter and a half of England is urbanised.[8] In fact, 10% of England is urban, with around 5% of land devoted to housing. Emotive headlines, driven by that lobby, scream of a green and pleasant land at risk of being 'concreted over'. It is a great deception.

The Campaign to Protect Rural England (CPRE), a well-funded campaigning group, has commissioned research showing that councils have identified capacity for 'at least' 1 million homes on brownfield land, and that sites with planning permission alone can accommodate 450,000,[9] but this surely misses the point. As *The Economist* has noted, brownfield land is outrageously expensive to build on. It often needs a hefty public subsidy for remediation.[10] While no one wants to unnecessarily bulldoze England's prettiest countryside, it is delusional to argue that 'brownfield' offers an easy solution. In truth, we need a measured approach, balancing urban renewal in inner and outer cities with an acceptance that the pressures from rising household formation demand some well-planned new settlements, and modest village and town extensions.

How, then, did our housing model become so dysfunctional? The election of the late Lady (Margaret) Thatcher's Conservative government in 1979 certainly proved a turning point. It put social housing on a downward trajectory from which it has never recovered. In 1981, two years into her premiership, social housing – then, mainly provided by councils – made up 37.7% of housing stock, with 11.1% provided by private renters and 57.2% owner-occupied. By 2013, the figures were 17.3%, 17.4% and 65%, respectively.

In the 31 intervening years, around 2 million council homes were sold with generous discounts – pushing up home ownership in what turned out to be the biggest privatisation of all. However, in spite of a growing population – and promises by Lady Thatcher and her ministers – the government did not use the proceeds from council house sales to build more social homes. Thus, comparing Britain's dismal house-building record with other European countries during and after the 1980s, the late Peter Hall noted in a recent study that the major source of a building downturn was the 'drastic fall' in public housing completions during the 1980s – and, more recently, a similarly 'drastic fall' in private house-building since 2007/08.[11]

Revealingly, in today's broken market, the private rented sector – which includes former council housing, since resold to private landlords – has now overtaken social housing, while the level of home-ownership is stalling, particularly in London – and for the young, it is falling. The annual English housing survey reported in February 2015 that outright owner-occupiers (7.4 million) now exceeded those with a mortgage for the first time (6.9 million). Meanwhile, the proportion of 25–34 year olds buying a home has fallen: from nearly two thirds to just 36% in 10 years. Yet, demand for social housing is strong; the estimated 1.7 million low-income people, and families, languishing on council house waiting lists are testament to that.

As others have noted, these latest figures highlight the extreme generational inequality of our broken housing market; difficulties in buying a home, and a lack of social housing, have pushed the young into often substandard, insecure housing. Now, half of 25–34 year olds rent privately. The National Housing Federation succinctly explains the dilemma: first-time buyers now have to pay, in real terms, 10 times the deposit that was needed in the early 1980s: 'Home ownership is becoming an exclusive members' club', it warned; 'Only the wealthiest of the next generation will be able to buy a home if current trends continue.'[12]

However, there is another way. With political will, governments – of which more shortly – could follow the example of previous administrations and introduce mechanisms to deliver more homes on a scale and at a cost to meet the needs of Britain, particularly England. That means finding land. With forward planning – as the record of the UK's 28 new towns shows – the state even gets a generous payback.

Rather than encouraging home ownership at any cost, the 2010–15 government should have recognised the reality of a changing market and the need for many more homes across types and tenures, particularly genuinely affordable ones. Yet, as the Lincolnshire experience shows, even modest measures to address this area – the obligation for builders to provide a relatively small number of affordable homes in each

Affordable and private housing under construction at Crosby Ravensworth, in Cumbria. Rural building is falling as demand is rising

development – were whittled away, then effectively scrapped, by the government in England.

As David Orr, Chief Executive of the National Housing Federation, laments, we now seem locked into a "sense of inevitability … that there is no other course … it is what we have come to accept".[13] We must break out of this cycle of decline – yes, sometimes despair – with some incremental steps:

• First, the case for ending generous tax breaks is so overwhelming that governments should move swiftly to bring a sense of order to the land market. It delivers windfalls for a few at the expense of the many unable to find a secure home to buy or to rent. George Dunn, Chief Executive of the Tenant Farmers' Association, rightly points out that 100% relief from inheritance tax, which has fuelled a farmland buying spree – and, in turn, has ratcheted up the price of building land – represents a massive state subsidy. If for no other reason, we must act to stop the excesses of the London housing market spilling into our rural acres – now seen by this moneyed elite as a safer investment bet, capable of overriding any future property downturn, if they can get their hands on this increasingly scarce resource: our land. Let us be clear, the consequences of aggressive land trading, pushing up the cost of developments, means either smaller homes crammed onto high-density, poorly connected, estates, or larger detached housing – 'McMansions', in the planning vernacular of the US – on larger developments.

- Second, tried and tested measures, which have already delivered hundreds of thousands of homes, should be reintroduced using new town legislation still on the statute book. Well-planned, carbon-efficient, new and renewed communities are needed rather than the serried ranks of soulless, standardised 'boxes' littering our landscape – the antithesis of planning. In this area, at least, we are repeating the mistakes of the past. In the words of one leading housing expert, familiar with the mortgage market: "The worry is that, in any downturn, some of these new houses are so small, on marginal sites, that they will lose value and put people into negative equity."

- Third, local councils – and groups of authorities – must be given a leading role in assembling and, where necessary, buying land in cooperation with a national government through the (English) Homes and Communities Agency, whose role diminished under the 2010–15 UK government. This could involve a forward-funding model – inevitably, through central government investment – to kick-start land assembly and to prepare sites for new housing. It is a tried and tested 'carrot and stick' procedure, with the added benefit of compulsory purchase powers available when necessary. It was used by a string of limited-life urban development corporations created by the Conservative government in the

1980s and 1990s, from London Docklands, to Liverpool, Tyneside, Central Manchester and Leeds. The National Housing Federation, representing not-for-profit housing associations – now the only significant suppliers of affordable housing – has suggested that councils should develop 'local land strategies' to assemble both public and private sector land and to prepare it for development. Currently, it cautions that government departments, substantial landowners in their own right, have to meet individual targets for land disposal, with no bearing on strategic needs.

Most of all, to make any progress, we need proactive planning, rather than the current, deregulatory free-for-all. We should seek inspiration from past achievements. The 28 UK new towns, with a population of 2.6 million by 2001, may have their detractors. However, at their best, they provided a model for truly sustainable communities – with Letchworth Garden City (see Chapter One) a forerunner. It should inspire us today.

Although the term 'garden city' was invoked by the 2010–15 government, it was far from clear whether seemingly enthusiastic ministers, including Prime Minister David Cameron, had absorbed its collectivist ethos, namely, taking control of land and using an uplift in its value as development progressed to benefit the community. In Letchworth, for instance, the residual assets of the original development company have been incorporated into a city heritage foundation, a self-funding charitable organisation that reinvests its income for long-term community benefit.[14]

Letchworth, and its successor, Welwyn Garden City, provided the model for the 28 new towns built in two phases from 1948 through to the 1970s and 1980s. They were financed by 60-year fixed loans from the government, from 3% to 16% in the 1970s. However, in spite of this progressively heavy interest, they still repaid 57% of the costs to the Treasury, and the first new towns repaid their loans 30 years 'early' – ironically, triggering penalty payments – and even leant money to other bodies.

John Walker, now a consultant, was chief executive of the Commission for New Towns (CNT) from 1992 to 1999, which assumed new town assets and repaid loans of £4 billion to the government. Before that, he was planning director of Milton Keynes – the last new town to be designated – for 12 years. Walker remains an evangelist for the new town model. He remembers land for the new town being bought (with a government loan) from owners at 'existing use' (farming) value, under threat of compulsory purchase: "It was rarely needed ... the value created [from the uplift in value from development] meant we could easily repay the loans."[15] Indeed, he recalls handing over a cheque for the final Milton Keynes repayment of £100 million to a government minister in 1997, which included a £20 million penalty charge for an early payback.

John Lewis, a former senior director of the government's Homes and Communities Agency who is now chief executive of Letchworth Garden City Heritage Foundation, argues strongly for a continued government role: "The state commits itself to funding road and rail schemes, when a payback is questionable, yet there's a reluctance when it comes to a basic need – housing – with a guaranteed return which the big infrastructure schemes don't offer", he says. "It doesn't make sense."[16]

However, if the state is now reluctant to take the long view and forward-fund, can we learn from other models of community initiative and ownership? As we shall see, vibrant communities – rather than state institutions – are now filling a vacuum by taking over land, building homes and renewing villages and neighbourhoods through local endeavour – albeit, on a modest scale.

Notes

[1] Ruskin, J. (1865) 'Sesame and lilies', Lecture 2, 'Of Queen's Gardens'.

[2] Gambba-Jones, R. (2015) 'Compounding the homes crisis', *First*, no 582, 14 February.

[3] KPMG and Shelter (2015) 'Building the homes we need'. Available at: www.thehomesweneed.org.uk

[4] Lyons, M. (2014) 'The Lyons housing review', October.

[5] Munton, R., 'Rural land ownership in the UK: changing patterns and future possibilities for land use', *Land Use Policy*. Available at: www.elsevier.com/locate/landusepol

[6] See: www.gov.uk/government/statistical-data-sets/live-tables-on-house-building

[7] Home Builders Federation, 'Big jump in number of new homes started'. Available at: info@hbf.co.uk

[8] See: www.ipsos-mori.com/Assets/Docs/Polls/SRI_IpsosMORIBPFtopline_080512.PDF

[9] CPRE (2014) 'From wasted space to living spaces', 24 November. Available at: www.cpre.org.uk

[10] *The Economist* (2013) 'The blighty Britain, the brownfield illusion', 2 May. Available at: www.economist.com

[11] Hall, P. (2014) *Good cities, better lives*, London: Routledge.

[12] National Housing Federation, 'Broken market, broken dreams'. Available at: www.housing.org.uk/publications/browse/home-truths-2014

[13] Orr, D., interviewed January 2015.

[14] See: www.letchworth.com/heritage-foundation

[15] Walker, J., interviewed December 2014.

[16] Lewis, J., interviewed December 2014.

SEVEN

Villages and neighbourhoods rising

You say you want a revolution ... we all want to change the world.[1]

Barely a month after the 2010 UK general election, revolution was in the air – for one member of the new government, at least. The then Housing Minister, Grant Shapps, invoked 'revolution' as his watchword. He went local. It did not last.

Out went national and regional housing targets; he dismissed them as 'Stalinist'. In came a laissez-faire regime in which communities, rather than government, would decide what was to be built, and where. It proved a high-risk strategy.

Never a man to miss the opportunity for a quick headline, Shapps was the star billing at the annual conference of England's community land trusts (CLTs) late in June 2010.[2] These small, largely village-based charities – now extending their reach into cities – had already delivered scores of affordable homes. They were warmly embraced by the new minister, underlining a brave new world of localism. Best of all, the theme chimed with the short-lived, high-profile, yet ill-defined 'Big Society' agenda of David Cameron.

Still savouring his new-found role in government, Shapps told the CLT delegates:

"In opposition, I said … we would start a revolution where communities would get involved in providing homes for themselves. Today, it's time to start that revolution. For the first time, it will be communities – not central government – who decide what happens in their local area."[3]

New legislation heralded more local powers, with the prospect of neighbourhood plans, in theory, offering community control over land use. The government, through its Homes and Communities Agency, even ring-fenced £25 million over four years from 2011 to support house-building through CLTs.

Enthusiasm soon waned. In the subsequent four-year spending round, no money was ring-fenced for funding. CLTs appeared sidelined. Shapps had moved on to become the Conservative Party chairman, its chief spokesman for a period. Nevertheless, with

New developments, like this, mix homes for affordable renting and self-build plots, where people acquire land from a community trust and then employ a builder.

this dedicated government fund ending, CLTs are still expanding, particularly in the South-West, Eastern England and the North-West. Key to their success is getting land at a low price – sometimes gifted by councils at below-market rates – and then fund-raising through borrowing and, perhaps, through issuing shares to raise cash to begin either building directly or by partnering with housing associations. Sometimes, the new homes are complemented by other facilities, such as village halls, small workshops and children's nurseries.

What began as a modest venture by three locals in the Oxfordshire village of Stonesfield in 1983 has now grown into a national movement of at least 170 CLTs in England alone, 60 of which are actively developing housing. So far, they have built around 500 homes; by 2020, the CLT Network, a national charity, estimates that 3,000 will be completed. However, with more support from a seemingly detached government, Catherine Harrington, the CLT Network's enthusiastic director, says that they could build 9,000 homes.

Amid the hectic market in land trading, outlined in Chapter Six, Harrington says that CLTs are highlighting one overarching issue: an acute shortage of social and affordable homes marginalising a whole (younger) generation, "and a lot of that is down to the land market".[4]

The availability of land, sometimes gifted on condition that it is used only for affordable homes – for rental or for owner-occupation – is clearly the key. Typically, a CLT keeps the freehold, putting a resale restriction on a property in order to retain its affordability and to ensure that it does not fall into private ownership. There is another important ingredient: like a garden city, such as Letchworth, the CLT captures any increase in land value for community benefit. Ask Harrington if the government should be doing more to bring down the cost of land – and, hence, housing – and she quickly responds: "Yes, absolutely. They have ignored the land question for far too long."[5]

In Stonesfield, as in other areas, from Oxfordshire to Cumbria, Devon and Cornwall, the community concerns had a familiar ring, namely, grossly inflated property markets putting houses way beyond the reach of locals on average incomes. By 1990, the Stonesfield CLT had completed six affordable homes on a quarter-acre site. The granting of planning approval alone had raised the value from £3,250 to £150,000 – providing security for a bank loan. Investors were offered a 3% return. Donations rolled in.

Today, the CLT owns 15 homes, the local post office and a pre-school group. It has put money into the local primary school. Tony Crofts, one of its founders, says that they not only successfully raised money, but have also paid off loans, achieved a healthy surplus and have assets of £3 million: "We have showed what can be done", he enthuses, idealism undimmed. "We are striving to build a new, stable society, not based on speculation. To hell with the banks and the government – let's build our own economy."[6]

If the movement has not quite reached those heady ideals, progress nationally has been steady. Crofts feels that cash should not necessarily be a problem for emerging CLTs: "There's a lot of good money around looking for a home", he maintains.[7] It is a sentiment shared by David Brown, who chairs the High Bickington Community Property Trust in Devon, one of the country's most ambitious CLTs. It has built 16 affordable homes, a new community centre and four workshops, and created 14 new allotments; it also has ambitious to turn a large barn into housing with attached workshops. Fifteen private houses are planned to support the affordable housing and help pay off loans.[8]

However, it has been a hard slog for Brown, a retired social work professional, and the local volunteers. Interviewing him first in 2009, he told me: "We are coming back to the stage where people want to look after their own areas, taking the role of the old local squire ... who controlled everything."[9] Affordable land – in the form of a Devon County Council-owned farm coming to the end of a tenancy – was the key to unlocking a relatively large development in the village (population 700). The council sold it to the new CLT for a nominal sum.

What, then, can we learn from the triumphs, trials and tribulations of CLTs in England? First, they need a long-term commitment from a Westminster government. It should learn from the experience of Scotland, where a Highlands Small Communities Housing Trust benefits from (Scottish-only) legislation allowing housing providers to get designated land at a discount provided that it is only ever used for affordable housing. The Scottish government also provides low-interest loans.

Second, short-term political gimmicks – be they 'Big Society' or other empty slogans – are no substitute for a long-term commitment through grants and soft loans underpinned by continuing political support. Take the vibrant village of Crosby Ravensworth in Cumbria, set in the rolling farmland of the Eden Valley, below the Hartside summit and between the North Pennines and the Lake District.[10] Portrayed as the living embodiment of Cameron's 'Big Society', it received visits from the prime minister, his ministers and senior civil servants during the early days of the last government. Its CLT also – crucially – got a £666,000 grant from the government's Homes and Communities Agency to deliver 12 affordable homes just before the Chancellor George Osborne slashed funds for affordable housing in England by half shortly after the 2010 general election.

Ministers enthused about the success of Crosby Ravensworth, which probably gained the highest profile of four original 'Big Society' pilots. On one visit, the former Minister for Civil Society, Nick Hurd, hailed it as emblematic of "ambitious and tenacious villagers standing up and saying 'We will do this ourselves.'"[11]

The CLT is well on the way to selling seven private building plots to help cut its overdraft – a necessary, if onerous, burden that underlines the financial challenges facing CLTs. Cynically, you might say that they served a political purpose for the last government, however briefly, before ministers either lost interest or moved on.

In reality – whatever the heady, revolutionary talk of Grant Shapps in 2010 – these CLTs can never address the scale of a housing crisis in which rural house-building in England fell to an average of 2,374 new homes annually during the lifetime of the last government.[12] The previous Labour administration did slightly better, averaging 2,902 a year – still well below demand of at least 7,500 annually, according to the Rural Housing Policy Review of February 2015. In short, actions speak louder than words.

Notes

[1] The Beatles (1968) *The white album*, Lennon–McCartney.

[2] CLT Network, see: www.communitylandtrusts.org.uk

[3] Shapps, G., speech to the CLT national conference, June 29 2010. Available at: https://westkengibbsgreen.wordpress.com/political-support/

[4] Harrington, C., interviewed April 2015.

[5] Harrington, C., interviewed April 2015.

[6] Hetherington, P. (2009) 'The rise of community-owned land', *The Guardian*, 8 April. Available at: www.theguardian.com

[7] Hetherington, P. (2009) 'The rise of community-owned land', *The Guardian*, 8 April. Available at: www.theguardian.com

[8] High Bickington Community Property Trust Ltd, see: www.highbickington.org

[9] Hetherington, P. (2009) 'The rise of community-owned land', *The Guardian*, 8 April. Available at: www.theguardian.com

[10] Hetherington, P. (2011) 'Our community pub would have opened with or without Big Society', *The Guardian*, 5 July. Available at: www.theguardian.com

[11] Hetherington, P. (2011) 'Our community pub would have opened with or without Big Society', *The Guardian*, 5 July. Available at: www.theguardian.com

[12] Rural Housing Policy Review (2015) 'A fair deal for rural communities', February. Available at: www.hastoe.com/fairdeal

EIGHT

Highlands and Islands rising

Ye see yon birkie, ca'd a lord
Wha struts an' stares, an' a' that;
Tho' hundreds worship at his word
He's but a coof for a' that.[1]

When Robert Burns lampooned the aristocracy in his masterly song evoking the dignity of all men, regardless of birth and wealth, the Highlands were in ferment. What became known as the Clearances – the brutal removal of families from their modest, stone homes to make way for sheep – unleashed a lingering bitterness. It is etched deeply in the collective psyche of many Scots.

From an English perspective, the powerful emotions aroused by this dark period in Scottish history 200 years ago seem to barely register. It is still sometimes portrayed as the British establishment versus the Highland masses through the all-powerful lairds, or landed class. It also generates an enduring sense of injustice – much stronger than any emotional fallout from the Enclosures (see Chapter Two) – and a continuing need to right some terrible wrongs by addressing the use, abuse and, crucially, the ownership of land.

Significantly, when a seemingly radical Scottish National Party (SNP) government late in 2014 promised another round of land reform, ministers evoked 'historical baggage' – a euphemism for the Clearances – to put their case into context. Central to this is the oft-quoted estimate from the land reform campaigner Andy Wightman that 432 owners account for 50% of privately held land in Scotland. Furthermore, 83% of the country's land is held privately, with the remainder owned by public organisations such as the Forestry Commission, the Scottish government and the (soon-to-be-devolved) Scottish element of the Crown Estate.[2]

Likewise, sections of the landowning class similarly evoked 'historical baggage', albeit pejoratively, when, to their horror, the SNP government subsequently laid out its land reform agenda. It wants legislation:

- to intervene if the scale of landownership, and the conduct of a landowner, is considered a 'barrier to sustainable development';
- to establish a permanent Land Reform Commission to maintain momentum, while strengthening the ability of tenant farmers to buy their holdings;
- to amend the rights of succession so that landowners can no longer leave their estates to a single heir, bringing Scotland into line with European countries that adopted Napoleonic codes after the French Revolution; and
- to reintroduce business rates on sporting estates to help fund a doubling of community landownership, from 500,000 to 1 million acres, and thus create a 'fairer and more equitable' distribution of land.

All this is in marked contrast to a quiescent England, where (as discussed in Chapter One) even a rational debate about land use – let alone the case for government intervention – is proving elusive. But for how long? Surely the pressures, and the threats, facing our shared island, and the exploitation of land for tax breaks – outlined in earlier chapters – transcend national boundaries. As noted previously, this

Scottish coastline: the Crown Estate owns half the Scottish foreshore and all the seabed. Its responsibilities in Scotland are being passed to the Scottish Government.

is underlined by the first flotation on the stock market of a farming company, Greenshields Agri – based in Edinburgh, but registered in the Isle of Man – in the spring of 2015. With land on both sides of the border, it has made a direct pitch to investors to reap the benefits of a boom in UK farmland.[3]

As Richard Lochhead, the senior Scottish government minister driving through land reform, reminded me, 85% of Scotland's land is classed as 'marginal' and, hence, unsuitable for growing crops – "entirely the opposite of England", he says.[4] England, of course, has some of the UK's best farmland. As outlined in Chapter Three, it is capable of being more productive. We are, in short, interdependent in so many ways. We share the same island and depend on the same food retailers – and, hence, the same farms – while farming concerns, as noted, transcend the border. Yet, the ideological and philosophical gulf between a new Conservative UK government, laissez-faire in outlook, and an interventionist, social-democratic-inclined SNP administration, highlighted at the 2015 Oxford Farming Conference, was wide before the 2015 election – and clearly still is.[5]

Whether the Scottish reform initiative will prompt a more searching analysis of land use throughout the UK remains to be seen. However, the landowners I have interviewed fear that a reformist groundswell building up behind reform in Scotland could conceivably spill over the border. Might it, perhaps, prompt a more serious analysis of land use among centre-left parties, such as elements of Labour and the powerful SNP group now in Westminster, for instance?

Overall, the proposed land reforms will cost the Scottish government little, but the political payback might be significant. Cynics have argued that they deliver the SNP a popular cause to exploit at minimal expense, but they are nonetheless welcome, prompting, as we shall see, not only soul-searching by the organisation representing the large landed estates, but also innovative forms of alternative ownership.

Protests, so far, have been predictable: opponents warn of a looming 'class war' and of an over-mighty state bearing down on private property, deterring investment and threatening jobs. One ludicrous headline even warned of 'socialist-style collectivisation'; the very antithesis of what is proposed.[6] However, the arguments have certainly added spice to an intensifying debate. The lobby group Scottish Land and Estates (SLE) – formerly the Scottish Landowners' Federation – launched a 'Landowners Charter' early in 2015, both to challenge the Scottish government's reform package and to try to present itself as an enlightened organisation rather than one mindlessly defending an old order.[7] The charter's four principles – namely, 'for all landowners to be open, inclusive, enabling and responsible' – underline their concern about the excesses of some estates tarnishing the collective image of Scottish landowning.

Nevertheless, David Johnstone, the SLE chairman, went on the offensive against the SNP: "There are those who take great delight in stigmatising private landownership regardless of the overwhelming evidence of the positive contribution we make", he maintained.[8] However, Johnstone, a youthful 40-something who owns and manages his family's 12,000-acre Annandale Estate in Dumfries and Galloway, acknowledges shortcomings by some – unnamed – landlords: "Time and again we are reminded that the admirable efforts of the majority of landowners are undermined by a minority who make little or no effort to engage with their communities."

It is a sentiment shared by Richard Scott, 10th Duke of Buccleuch and Queensberry, who heads the UK's largest private landholding. In 1999, his father, the 9th Duke, asked me pointedly when a few 'bad apples' in the landowning class should lead to a wholesale onslaught on the big estates.[9] His son is equally forthright, being critical of the minority yet viewing the prospect of further reform legislation with such dismay that he even questioned whether they should remain as substantial Scottish landowners: "It's quite an impasse moment ... but if it doesn't work out for the better I can't see us seeing it's sensible to hang on in there, owning huge amounts of land", he added in an interview late in 2014.[10]

We meet in the splendid library of Bowhill, a Georgian-cum-classical mansion among the gentle hills and woodlands of the Scottish borders, near the town of Selkirk, and one of the family's three stately homes. We ranged over Richard Scott's family history, the traditions of his forebears and the perception of duty to the many communities embraced by the substantial holdings of Buccleuch estates: 240,000 acres, mainly in Scotland, plus a chunk of Northamptonshire. These extensive lands, he reminds me, halved in size during the last century after Lloyd George's assault on inherited wealth.

The biggest, like the Buccleuchs, survived: "I am very lucky to have had forebears who were fascinated developing their estates, deeply attached to the land, but always wanting to move it forward", he volunteers. He acknowledged that he was, possibly, the last in the line: "We are at a pivotal moment", he sighed; "If we were talking in five years' time and the estate had shrunk by a quarter I wouldn't be surprised. I think I would go that far." Did he feel threatened? "Yes. In saying that, I recognise there are people on the other side of the land debate – Andy Wightman and so on – who have been campaigning for most of their lives, and most of my life, who will be pleased to hear that."

This is Burns' music to the ears of land reformer Andy Wightman[11] and to Richard Lochhead. The minister maintains that landowners who do not frustrate the ambitions of communities have nothing to fear: "However, any reasonable person would look at Scotland and recognise that the concentrated pattern of landownership – indeed, Europe's most extreme – can be an obstacle to economic development and people and communities having a say over their own destiny", Lochhead contends. "It is also a concentration of power and wealth that should be shared." He talks of a rolling programme of radical measures being framed in a series of bills that will enable communities to buy abandoned or neglected land – in rural as well as urban areas – and to "equip ministers to intervene on ownership and management that can range from potential enforced sales to instructing certain actions to be taken". It seems uncompromising language.

For land reform campaigners, activist government rarely comes better than this. Andy Wightman argues that if more people have a stake in land, they will have a much higher commitment to use it in the public interest. This, in turn, will lead to greater accountability, 'democratic engagement and higher levels of productivity'.

The gulf between the landed and the landless, in short, is as wide as a (continuing) divide over the Highland Clearances. It is still portrayed by apologists – including one significant landowner interviewed – as a misunderstood episode that 'reformed' land use and delivered meat and wool to the burgeoning cities of the Industrial Revolution. This violent period is evoked in many a long walk across a wild and spectacular landscape. Ruins of abandoned townships provide a vivid testament to the destruction of a whole settlement pattern, still seen by some as an early version of 'ethnic cleansing' before the term gained common currency.

Now, sheep have largely disappeared. Much of the land is devoted to what is quaintly labelled 'field sports', namely, stalking for majestic red deer, with other shooting (for game birds) and fishing thrown in. Often labelled 'Europe's last wilderness', the Highlands have thus

After the kill: deer stalking in the Highlands, in part a playground for the global super-rich. Source: Murdo Macleod

become a vast adventure playground for the European and Middle-Eastern rich, and occasionally famous: their vast estates, literally, liquid assets, sometimes owned by absentee landlords and valued by land agents according to a formula tied to both the levels of salmon caught and the numbers of red deer shot on the hills.

Back in the 19th century, when Britain was probably the richest nation in the world, Queen Victoria's personal purchase of Balmoral on Deeside (25,000 acres) made owning a sporting estate 'supremely fashionable amongst the super-rich ... estates changed hands for eye-watering sums'[12] – and they still can. In this rich persons' playground, outsiders hold half of all estates – Arabs, Russians, Scandinavians, Americans and all – often fuelling resentment among locals. Indeed, a Danish textiles billionaire, Anders Holch Povlsen, has amassed an acreage of 150,000 acres, becoming the second-biggest private landowner behind the Duke of Buccleuch.

Why the allure? First, Scotland is one of the few places where overseas buyers can get as much land as they want with few questions asked apart from the imperative of ready cash. Second – as discussed previously – estates are exempt from inheritance tax after two years if land is used nominally for agriculture. Third, Britain's system of land registration, in which owners can hide their identity, is attractive to overseas buyers keen to avoid tax in their home country. As *Scottish Field* magazine observed in March 2015, this explains why officialdom only knows who owns 26% of the land – for the time being. Richard Lochhead has promised a 10-year programme to thoroughly register all land – under Scotland's distinctly different legal system – "so the owner will be easy to identify".

Although pressure for legislation to vigorously pursue land reform has been building up for much of the last century, the re-establishment of a Scottish Parliament in 1999 provided an opportunity for action. The then Labour First Minister, the late and redoubtable Donald Dewar, laid the foundations for the Land Reform (Scotland) Act 2003 before he died. It effectively gave communities first refusal when estates come on the market – to the alarm of a once-dominant landowning class. Although community buyouts of several large estates preceded the legislation, almost 500,000 acres – mainly in the Highlands and Islands – is now owned by local communities, the vast majority (95%) on 17 large estates bought with help from a Scottish Land Fund, lottery funding, charities and local fund-raising.[13]

Richard Lochhead says that 18 applications for community ownership, under Dewar's legislation, have progressed successfully while a further three are currently being considered. They range from large tracts of the Highlands and the Western Isles – where a majority of land in the 120-mile archipelago is now community-owned – to smaller undertakings. Several community buyouts preceded Dewar's legislation: the small island of Eigg, in the inner Hebrides 10 miles from the mainland, is one classic exemplar.

After years of insecurity and neglect, the Isle of Eigg Heritage Trust bought the island for £1.5 million in June 1997 after an international fund-raising appeal. The transformation since then has been remarkable: houses on the small island have been renovated, a new multipurpose centre – embracing a post office, shop and tearoom – has been built; the population has risen from 60 to 90; and a fast broadband network has been installed. An island electricity grid integrates four wind turbines, three micro-hydroelectric schemes and a string of solar panels in order to provide round-the-clock power. Locals use portable 'smart meters' to monitor usage, which is 'capped' at 5 kilowatts per household.[14]

Island of Eigg, overlooking the neighbouring island of Rhum, bought by islanders in 1997. Source: Murdo Macleod

With seven children now attending the island school, and a further five at secondary school on the mainland, Maggie Fyffe, Secretary of the Heritage Trust, says that secure ownership has encouraged locals to return and others to set up home amid the rugged beauty of Eigg. It measures 5.6 by 3 miles at the widest point: "Quite a lot of people [including her own daughter] are returning because things are happening, work is available, and we are providing more plots for housing." Perhaps, most significantly, the success of Eigg, which lies just south of Skye, has provided a momentum for other community buyouts.

The population of Eigg is rising. Inhabitants enjoy a community-owned local
electricity grid powered by renewables – wind, solar and hydro.
Source: Murdo Macleod

Ownership, of course, can take different forms. Further north, in
Wester Ross, former senior Whitehall civil servant Richard Munday
and his wife, Claire, are planning to gradually hand 4,000 acres to the
local community around the village of Shieldaig. The Mundays, who
moved to Scotland in 1993, are establishing a Charitable Land Trust,
which will initially include the couple and their two children. Richard
Munday supports the Scottish government's reform agenda. He says
that across huge tracts of the Highlands, absentee landowners – with
some exceptions – are "insensitive to the views of local people".[15]

Fifteen years after Donald Dewar's groundbreaking initiative,
Scotland's new First Minister, Nicola Sturgeon (as noted in Chapter
One), in her first speech to the Scottish Parliament, pointedly evoked

Dewar's spirit: "Scotland's land must be an asset that benefits the many, not the few."[16] Parting company with the laissez-faire approach of the Westminster government, Sturgeon told Members of the Scottish Parliament (MSPs) that her SNP administration would legislate before the next parliamentary elections in 2016 to give ministers powers to intervene where the "scale of landownership or the conduct of a landlord is acting as a barrier to sustainable development".

As part of the reform process, measures to speed up land registration in Scotland and make ownership more transparent – throwing some light onto the opaque world of 'beneficial' ownership – will be introduced. Business rate exemptions, which have applied on sporting estates since 1994, will be removed. Proceeds will be used to boost a Scottish Land Fund – which helps communities buy and manage land – from £3 million in 2014 to a projected £10 million from 2016. The aim is to double community landownership to one million acres by 2020. Significantly, the SNP government wants to extend its land reform programme into urban Scotland in order to give neighbourhoods a stake in regeneration programmes in towns and cities, and to encourage local groups to help kick-start renewal programmes – potentially using community-owned land as collateral against which to borrow.

In many ways, the passion of Scottish land reformers echoes that of Lloyd George a century earlier, when the reach of a UK government extended into Scotland. Interviewed in the Scottish Parliament, Richard Lochhead – the senior minister, or cabinet secretary, overseeing land reform – was undaunted by the criticisms from both landowners and Scottish Conservatives: "Land is a national resource", he insisted:

"A country depends on land to grow food, produce energy, give us water for leisure, health and wellbeing, to live and work on – and that's why it's in the public interest for land to work for all the people of Scotland and not just a few people."

It is a sentiment that, for now, we are unlikely to hear from a UK government, which oversees England. Rarely has the gulf between neighbouring nations appeared so wide.

Notes

[1] Burns, R. (1795) 'A man's a man for a' that'.

[2] Wightman, A., 'Land matters', Available at: www.andywightman.com

[3] See: www.greenshieldsagri.com

[4] Lochhead, R., interviewed February 2015.

[5] Oxford Farming Conference, January 2015, see: www.ofc.org.uk

[6] *The Telegraph* (2013) 'Lairds warn against dividing up Scotland's estates', 1 August. Available at: www.telegraph.co.uk

[7] See: www.scottishlandandestates.co.uk

[8] Johnstone, D., interviewed January 2015, at Allandale Estates office, Dumfries and Galloway.

[9] Hetherington, P. (1999) 'Laird of 250,000 acres warns of false utopias', *The Guardian*, 6 January.

[10] Scott, R., Duke of Buccleuch and Queensberry, interviewed October 2014 at Bowhill, Scottish Borders.

[11] Wightman, A., 'Land matters', Available at: www.andywightman.com

[12] *Scottish Field* (2015) 'Making sense of land reform', March. Available at: www.scottishfield.co.uk

[13] Land Reform Review Group (2014) 'The land of Scotland and the common good', 23 May. Available at: www.gov.scot/Publications/2014/05/2852

[14] See: www.isleofeigg.net

[15] Munday, R., interviewed February 2015.

[16] Sturgeon, N. (2014) 'Programme of government', Scottish Parliament, 16 November. Available at: http://news.scotland.gov.uk/Speeches-Briefings/First-Minister-Programme-for-Government

NINE

Will England rise?

Land and its many uses provides a bedrock for the country and the foundation for our wellbeing, prosperity, and national identity.[1]

Several weeks before the UK general election in May 2015, scores of radical land reformers met in the House of Commons to debate the future of our most basic resource. With the political parties generating more heat than light in the main debating chamber, the 'People's Parliament' – an ad hoc, disparate assembly organised by the Labour MP John McDonnell – packed into a nearby committee room. To the question 'Whose land is our land?', there was one collective answer: 'It's ours'.

Squatters, folk singers, housing campaigners and tenants all had their say. The little-known Labour Land Campaign flourished leaflets calling for specific economic policies to redress a fundamental flaw in the economy, namely, 'a denial of the importance of land ... the unjust powers in its "ownership" and the acceptance of land wealth as unearned income for the owners'.[2]

If the proceedings were somewhat anarchic, the message from some was profound. As the main speaker, writer and campaigner

Kevin Cahill observed: "The largest number of [UK] land owners own the smallest amount of land."[3] In short, home-owners – under 70% of the population – collectively own a small slice of the UK classed as urban. That is well under 10 per cent of the land mass.

As Cahill noted, this demolishes the myth that the 60 million acres of our land is crowded; over 70%, after all, is 'agricultural' in its various forms – if not all prime farmland – with much of the remainder comprising mountain, bog and moorland. But how well managed is that 70%, our collective rural 'plot'? Cahill contends that it is in the self-interest of the minority who own what he calls the 'green patches' – the countryside – to peddle the myth to the great majority that our land is somehow overcrowded and unable to accommodate additional development.

In broader terms, this argument was well laid out in a 2010 Foresight report, *Land use futures*, from the Government Office for Science.[4] In considerable detail, it examined the future of land use in the UK over the next 50 years: 'Despite commonly-held public perceptions, much of the land of the UK remains undeveloped – around 90 per cent in the case of England', it contended. The report called for a reappraisal, presumably by government, to address major challenges – climate change (and, crucially, the implication for farming), demographic shifts and rising demand for housing – while making the obvious, yet profound, point that land provides the bedrock of the country and the foundation for our well-being and prosperity.

Yet, in the years since publication, inconveniently before the 2010 general election, no one in the government has taken its message sufficiently seriously to begin – at the very least – the necessary debate for that reappraisal of land use. The report has been shelved. A central message that the country is ill-prepared for the pressures ahead – housing and feeding the nation while addressing the challenges of climate change – proved politically inconvenient. As one member of a lead expert group of geographers, social scientists and economists charged with overseeing the project sighed: "No one in government wanted to hear. It was too big an issue to contemplate." So much so, in fact, that the group was apparently told to water down anything too contentious, such as the strong case for regional and strategic planning to coordinate, say, measures for climate change remediation and resilience.

The 2010 Conservative-led government had a visceral dislike of anything reeking of 'planning' to address the big issues of the day – such as coordinating flood defences across 30 separate planning authorities from the Thames to the Humber in order to address the threat of rising sea levels. As the Town and Country Planning Association[5] subsequently reported in 2012: "The relationship of sea level rises to food production in the east of England is one question that clearly cannot be delayed." But it has been.

My research during 2014–15 led to one inescapable conclusion: if we think about land at all, it is often in the narrow confines of our small patch (if we are fortunate to be among the diminishing number of home-owners) or about the perceived threat from 'development' on our doorsteps, sometimes more imagined than real. The bigger picture – housing and, crucially, feeding the people of our land – eludes a UK, particularly England, increasingly bereft of those collectivist societal ideals that infused the political class, across parties, in the 1950s and 1960s, my formative years.

In today's ultra-cautious, laissez-faire political climate, with ministers seemingly indifferent to the pressures facing our land, it might seem remarkable that a government had the vision to intervene in the interests of all the people with legislation to both open up the countryside after 1949 – courtesy of a National Parks and Access to the Countryside Act – and effectively 'nationalise' the right to develop land through the Town and Country Planning Act 1947, now mindlessly deconstructed. It was designed to bring a sense of order to our land, ending a 'you-want-it-you-build-it' development free-for-all.

As a nation, we had – still have, in many respects – much to celebrate. Surely, we should treasure our 15 national parks and ensure that we protect and maintain the almost 140,000 miles of footpaths – legal 'rights of way', after all – rather than tolerating their being run down, ever-more diminished by government spending cuts. Park budgets in England were slashed by up to 40% between 2010 and 2015, with hundreds of job losses, the closure of visitor centres and even some land sales: "The insidious and chaotic nature of the [government] cuts are bleeding the parks dry", complained the chief executive of the Campaign for National Parks.[6] Surely, a wake-up call? And what of our extensive footpath network in England and Wales, the envy of the world? Like the English planning system, it is similarly being run down; as any rambler or hill walker will attest, legal rights of way, dependent on signage and regular maintenance, are often poorly maintained as overall local authority budgets are slashed.

The impact of climate change provides another wake-up call. Early in 2015, plodging across the coastal marshes of Suffolk – sea defences still battered and, sometimes, broken by an extreme tidal surge late in 2013 – you cannot escape the impact of the forces of nature and our changing climate. Undoubtedly, this represents our greatest challenge. During that surge in neighbouring Norfolk, the waves leapt over coastal defences at Walcott and Happisburgh, pushing damaging salty

Hadrian's Wall path, 84 miles long. It became the 15th national trail when it opened in 2003. But many of our footpaths are increasingly poorly maintained.

water into an elaborate drainage network on which local farming depends. Further north in the county, looking towards the Wash from the vulnerable harbour-side at Wells-Next-The-Sea, where buildings were badly damaged during that surge, you are similarly aware of the potential threat to the nearby farmland, the most productive in the UK. It is only 62 years, after all, when a high spring tide driven by a severe storm engulfed the east coast of England as the water rose to six metres above the normal sea level, overwhelming the land. More than 300 people lost their lives in Suffolk and Essex.

Foresight's *Land use futures*, driven by hard evidence, pulled no punches. While 2.5 million acres – *only* 9% of our agricultural area – occupies flood plains, it embraces our best land: 57% of Grade 1 agricultural land (and 13% of Grade 2) alone. Some of this, of course, has been 'reclaimed' from the sea, and improved, over hundreds of years – 'an important asset in terms of national food security', according to the Foresight report. It put the capital value of 'at-risk' land at over £15 billion. The management of flood alleviation, and drainage, is therefore critical to maintaining domestic food production.

So, we have a choice, succinctly put neatly into perspective by Foresight's *Land use futures*: either governments provide high levels of

Flood defences in East Anglia: the government has been warned of the critical threat to our best farm land from rising sea levels.

flood protection to resist rising coastal threats, 'realigning defences', or they abandon large tracts to the sea. Presciently, it warned of the potential risk from rises in sea levels, and storm surges, in 2010 – three years before the last east-coast surge. Tom McCabe, executive director of community and environmental services at Norfolk County Council, vividly remembers that December 2013 tidal surge, which battered 50-year-old defences: "We were inches away from them going", recalls McCabe.[7] Like the National Audit Office (NAO) – public spending watchdog for the UK government – he is in no doubt that valuable farmland is extremely vulnerable.

In a report late in 2014, the NAO warned that millions of acres of farmland in England are potentially at risk of flooding because government spending on flood defences is being spread too thinly: about half of the country's defences – 1,356 schemes – are only being maintained to a minimal level. In 2009, the long-term investment strategy of the Environment Agency, the government body responsible for flood defences, warned that funding would need to rise by an average of £20 million a year, plus inflation, until 2035 in order to maintain the current level of risk. However, between 2010 and 2013, capital and revenue funding – for long-term investment and day-to-day maintenance – was cut by 18% and 10%, respectively.[8]

After the exceptional storms in the winter of 2013/14 – the wettest period in the south of England for 250 years – the government made an extra £270 million available under political pressure, thus reversing some of its own cuts. However, this was a reaction to publicity surrounding the flooding of the Somerset Levels – a coastal plain of around 170,000 acres (70,000 ha), drained by Dutch engineers in the 17th century – rather than to a wider threat in Eastern England and the more widespread tidal surges along its coastline late in 2013. Governments, in short, react with short-term measures rather than addressing the longer-term threat to our more productive acres in the East. As Amyas Morse, head of the NAO observed, the Environment Agency "will need to make difficult decisions about whether to continue maintaining assets in some areas or let them lapse".[9]

One inescapable conclusion emerges from interviews in 2014/15 with a range of players, from farmers, to landowners and council leaders charged with coordinating flood defences: the indifference of a government seemingly in self-denial, wedded to a complex cost–benefit analysis that puts the defence of property (one in six homes, for instance, at risk of flooding in England) ahead of farmland protection.

In a global economy, you might ask why self-sufficiency in basic foodstuffs is important, when, for instance, we import huge quantities of, say, green beans from East and North Africa, asparagus from Peru, and fruit and vegetables from Spain. In essence, that was the nub of a reply several years ago from a former secretary of state for environment, farming and rural affairs to a question from Norfolk farmer Louis Baugh: why this obsession with food self-sufficiency in a global market?

Concerned about the vicissitudes in this international market, Baugh recalls asking the then minister if the government of the day had a strategic food policy (this was Labour, before 2010). "I was told it did not matter where the food came from as long as it was ethically produced", recalls Baugh, who grows potatoes, cereals, sugar beet, green beans and maize (for beef cattle) on 1,000 acres of best Grade 1 and 2 land beside the Norfolk Broads.[10]

With all his land below the level of nearby rivers – and some below sea level – Baugh is concerned by the apparent indifference of governments to both flood defences and food security. He helped produce a 2010 report for the East Anglian National Farmers' Union (NFU),[11] warning of rising sea levels, tied to a wetter and warmer climate, taking a toll on the Broads and threatening 150 miles of clay and silt flood-bank defences that protect good farmland. It has already deteriorated.

Clearly, as a nation – seemingly complacent in the face of climate change and vulnerable sea defences – we should be doing more to exploit the potential of our land. By European standards, the farmed area of the UK (74%) is high. True, the number of farms has reduced by 50% since 1950 to about 230,000; on average, our commercial farms (as opposed to smallholdings and 'hobby farms' of a few acres) are now four times larger than the European Union (EU) average, with the biggest concentration in South and East England, where, as already noted, land trading often takes precedence over efficient farming, with crop production of secondary importance to capital appreciation and tax avoidance.

We can argue endlessly about the removal of hedgerows to produce large field systems, about an over-concentration of biofuel crops – such as oil seed rape – on land that might be used for food production, about the fragility of soils in future years through erosion from increasingly severe weather patterns, and about why the UK, once a world leader in farming research, is now tailing competitors such as Germany, Denmark, the Netherlands and New Zealand.[12]

However, in truth, we need an active government to oversee that most basic resource: our land. With little or no prospect of Scottish-style land reform legislation in England, at the very least, the case for a system of agreements, or 'compacts', between the government and landowners in order to create some certainty over land use – and to try and curb land abuse – is overwhelming.

Aside from a sometimes fevered market in land trading, in parts of the country, some big landowners are more potent planning agencies than local councils themselves, effectively determining the development process as powerful actors and sometimes exercising a negative power of veto. When these players are so influential, fundamental questions about the nature of local democracy need to be addressed. The rights of landowners, after all – both the new rich, institutions and those on estates inherited by a quirk of history courtesy of monarchical benevolence hundreds of years ago – surely have to be balanced by a wider responsibility to society, which rightly demands (or should?) that our land is a national resource on which we all ultimately depend.

If we rightly outlaw water pollution, rail against air pollution (some councils use by-laws to curb pollutants) and demand restrictions on the use of pesticides, surely it is time to turn our attention to the use – sometimes the abuse – of farmland, which attracts generous EU agricultural support. Surely, at the very least, a quid pro quo for this subsidy regime should be a legally binding code of conduct for UK farmland. If farmers sign up to agri-environment agreements to protect landscapes and habitats in return for subsidies – and the consequent oversight that involves – it should not represent a great leap of organisation to extend this principle to the good management of all their (and our) land.

As Philip Lowe, Professor of Rural Economy at Newcastle University says, farmers in receipt of EU farm payments should be obliged to sign up to basic principles of responsible land management "specifying their responsibilities to maintain the land in their care".[13] However, there is, of course, a broader issue at stake. If the last government, and previous administrations, claimed to have an 'active' industrial policy, for instance – no matter how questionable the reality – why has the case for an active land policy, overseeing our most basic resource for the benefit of all, eluded successive administrations? For starters, the plea to a new UK government from NFU President, Pembrokeshire farmer Meurig Raymond, for a national plan to increase the productive potential of farming should not fall on deaf ears.[14]

That should mark the start of a wider debate within government to address land – and the series of pressures it faces – in the fullest sense. Striking a balance between efficient farming, on the one hand, and managing the land and its fragile ecosystems and habitats, on the other, is not easy; providing the billions of pounds necessary to safeguard our best farming land from the impact of more extreme weather patterns might involve some hard choices in government priorities; reforming the tax system to ensure landowners pay their fair share of capital gains and inheritance tax, rather than avoiding it, will take political courage. However, we cannot continue as we are.

George Dunn, long-serving chief executive of the Tenant Farmers' Association and widely respected across the agricultural sector, is right to argue that the vast 'subsidy' given to buyers of farmland, in the form of inheritance tax and capital gains relief, serves the country extremely poorly. His words should ring alarm bells: "For those with a lot of cash, made through capital gains elsewhere in the economy, land provides the complete tax solution", he laments; "Roll money into land and … you run it as a 'sham' farming operation operated by another individual on a short-term basis. You take no risk. And when you pass away, there's all this tax relief."[15]

In short, someone in government urgently needs to start pulling the levers of fiscal reform. Yet, the ministry ostensibly in charge, the Department of the Environment, Food and Rural Affairs, does not control them, and the all-powerful Treasury – which does – has so far been either hostile or indifferent to any reform.

Howard Newby has forcefully argued that an "informed debate" about the future of rural Britain is urgently needed.[16] He was writing with some prescience in 1988 when the current pressures on our countryside – the need for more housing, the threat to our best farmland from climate change and rising sea levels, for instance – barely registered.

Once, governments, through various bodies such the Countryside Agency and the Commission for Rural Communities, viewed our land in a wider context beyond agriculture. However, since 2010, the government has abolished these bodies, which operated not only as ministerial advisers on rural policy, but also as critical friends.

Alarmingly, with the countryside – indeed, all England (and Britain) – facing unprecedented pressures on land and natural resources, no agency exists to lead that informed debate and develop an active land policy. We are approaching a collision of extremes – increasing demand for food, energy, water, housing – when we should be adapting to, and hopefully mitigating, the impact of climate change on that most basic resource: our land. But that means planning ahead, prioritising resources – and, yes, borrowing as a nation to invest in (and safeguard) our future – when the very concept of planning, still less long-term investment, has become a pejorative term. As things stand, we are vulnerable and ill-prepared. We could be doing so much better.

Notes

[1] Foresight (2010) *Land use futures; making the most of our land in the 21st century*, Government Office for Science, p 5.

[2] Labour Land Campaign, see: www.labourland.org

[3] People's Parliament, Committee room 15, House of Commons, 17 March 2015.

[4] Foresight (2010) *Land use futures; making the most of our land in the 21st century*, Government Office for Science.

[5] Town and Country Planning Association (2012) 'Lie of the land'. Available at: www.tcpa.org.uk/data/files/Lie_of_the_Land_ExecSummary.pdf

[6] Campaign for National Parks (2015) 'Stop the cuts to National Park Authority budgets', 27 March. Available at: www.cnp.org.uk

[7] McCabe, T., interviewed May, 2015.

[8] NAO (2014) 'Strategic flood risk management', 5 November. Available at: www.nao.org.uk/report/strategic-flood-risk-management-2

[9] NAO (2014) 'Strategic flood risk management', 5 November. Available at: www.nao.org.uk/report/strategic-flood-risk-management-2

[10] Baugh, L., interviewed March 2015.

[11] NFU East Anglia (2010) 'Farming and the Fens'. Available at: www.nfuonline.com/final-document

[12] Daneshkhu, S. (2015) 'Disturbing decline in food production', *Financial Times*, 24 February.

[13] Lowe, P., interviewed January 2015.

[14] NFU, 'Backing British farming in a volatile world'. Available at: www.nfuonline.com/635-15tl-the-report-digital-low-res/

[15] Dunn, G., interviewed February 2015.

[16] Newby, H. (1988) *The countryside in question*, Hutchinson.

Index

References to photos are shown in *italics*

A

Acquisition and Occupancy of
  Agricultural Land 56
agriculture *see* farming
Agriculture Acts (1947 & 1970)
  23, 28
Alnwick Castle 39–40, *41*, 47
aristocracy
  and breaking up of estates 46, 47,
    48
  critique of 47, 48
  Crown Estate 4, 14, 26, 43–5, *83*
  and Enclosures 15
  extent of landownership 52
  Grosvenor Group 49–51
  Holkham Estate 47, 48–9, 59
  interwar years 22
  justification of inheritance 41–2,
    48–9, 50–1
  and land reform 18–19, 21, 46–7
  Northumberland Estates 39–43,
    46–7, 52
  our views of 46, 47
  resilience of 51
  in Scotland 21, 46–7
  see also individual aristocrats
Ashbrook, Kate 14
Attlee, Clement 22

B

Bainbridge, Simon 28–9
Baugh, Louis 99
Beedell, Jason 33, 34
Brown, David 78
brownfield land 66, 67
Buccleuch and Queensbury, 9th
  Duke of 48, 85
Buccleuch and Queensbury, 10th
  Duke of (Richard Scott) 4, 8–9,
  18–19, *45*, 46, 49, 85

C

Cahill, Kevin 15, 44, 56–7, 59–60,
  94
Campaign for National Parks 96
Campaign to Protect Rural
  England (CPRE) 67
Castle, Lady (Barbara) 20–1
Clearances (Highland) 81, 82, 86
Clery, Peter 15, 59, 60
climate change 96–9
Coalition Government (2010–15)
  see Conservative-led government
  (2010–15)
Coats, Charles 28
Coke family 47, 48–9, 59

Coke, Thomas (Earl of Leicester) 48–9
Common Agricultural Policy (EU) 34, 64
common land 14–16
community land trusts (CLTs) 75–9
community ownership in Scotland 88–91
Conservative Government (1979–97) 67, 70–1
Conservative Government (2015–) 83–4
Conservative-led Government (2010–15)
 and Defra cuts 9
 and farming 25–6, 35
 and flood defences 9, 95, 98–9
 and housing 8, 68, 70, 71, 75–6, 79
 and land ownership 16, 20, 21, 63
Cooperative Group 34
Cornwall, Duchy of 44
council houses 67–8
countryside
 changing nature of 7–8
 importance of 4–6
 romanticisation of 5, 6–8
Countryside and Rights of Way Act 2000 (England) 20
county council estate, and farm land 27–8
CPRE (Campaign to Protect Rural England) 67
Crofts, Tony 78
Crosby Ravensworth, Cumbria 69, 79
Crown Estate 4, 14, 26, 43–5, 83

D

death duties 22
Defra 9, 25–6, 32
Devon, CLTs 78
Dewar, Donald 88
Domesday Book 58
Domesday Book (Second) 52, 59–60
Duchy of Cornwall 44
Dunn, George 27, 30, 35, 69–70, 101
Dyson, James 35–6

E

Economist, The 67
Eigg, Isle of 88–9, 89, 90
Ellington Estate, Northumberland 44–5, 57
Ellis, Hugh 15–16, 52
Enclosures 14–16
Environment Agency 98
European Union, Common Agricultural Policy 34, 64
Eustice, George 35–6

F

Farmers' Guardian 30
farming
 attracting younger farmers 25–7, 31–2
 barriers to 25–8, 32
 and Coalition government (2010–15) 25–6, 35
 and county council estates 27–8
 crisis in 16
 and Defra 9, 25–6, 32
 and Enclosures 14–16
 and flooding 97–9
 and food production 31–3, 97, 99
 Greenshields Agri 34–5, 83

historically 14–16, 22, 23, 28, 58–9
importance of 31
and land ownership 18, 22, 26–8, 34–6, 56, 58–9, 69–70
National Farmers' Union (NFU) 32–3, 99, 101
and National Trust 18, 28–30
price of land 33–4, 69–70
and self-sufficiency 31, 32–3, 99
size of farms 99–100
and subsidies 23, 64, 100–1
and supply of land 33–4
and tax breaks 30, 69–70, 101–2
tenant farmers 26–30, 47–8
Tenant Farmers' Association (TFA) 27–8, 30, 35, 69–70, 101
yield improvements 31
Fewings, Andrew 26–7
field sports 86–7
flood defences 9, 95, 96–9, 97
food production, domestic 31–3, 97, 99
see also farming
footpaths 5, 20, 95, 96, 96
Foresight report 94–5, 97–8
Forestry Commission 3, 21
Fursdon, David 26, 32
future of land use 94–8
Fyffe, Maggie 89

G

Gambba-Jones, Roger 63, 64, 65, 66
garden cities 17, 71–2
Ghosh, Dame Helen 30
Gloucestershire, and county council estates 28
Greenshields Agri 34–5, 83

Grosvenor, Gerald Cavendish (Duke of Westminster) 49–51
Grosvenor Group 49–51

H

Hall, Peter 16–17, 67–8
Harrington, Catherine 77
Hartside Pass, Cumbria 1–2, 2
Henderson, Kate 15–16, 52
High Bickington Community Property Trust 78
Highlands Small Communities Trust 78–9
Hill, Octavia 17–18
Holkham Estate, Norfolk 47, 48–9, 59
home ownership 8, 68
Homes and Communities Agency (England) 70
housing
 affordable 68–72, 69, 75–9
 broken model of 66–9
 building downturn 67–8
 and Coalition government (2010–15) 8, 68, 70, 71, 75–6, 79
 community land trusts 75–9
 council houses 67–8
 and generational inequalities 68
 home ownership 8, 68
 and land prices 9–10, 63–4
 and new towns 70, 71–2
 private rented housing 68
 and role of local councils 70–1
 and 'shadow' market 64–5
 shortage of 66, 77, 79
 social housing 67–8
 suggested policies 69–72
 and supply of land 64–5
 and tax breaks 69–70
 where to build it 66–7
Hovesen, Poul 31, 33, 35

Howard, Ebenezer 17
Hunt, Tristram 18
Hurd, Nick 79

I

Isle of Eigg Heritage Trust
  88–9, *89, 90*

J

Johnstone, David 84–5
Jones, Ken 44–5

K

Kinder Scout 20
Kynaston, David 23

L

Labour governments/party 19,
  20, 22–3, 79, 88, 93–4, 99
land ownership, statistics 3–4, 8,
  51–2, 94
Land Reform (Scotland) Act
  2003 88
Land Registry 56–9, 60
land sales 35
land speculation 63, 64, 65
Land use futures 94–5, 97–8
landlords, National Trust 28–30,
  47–8
Landowners Charter, Scotland
  84
Laxton, North Nottinghamshire
  14
Leicester, Earl of (Thomas
  Coke) 48–9
Letchworth Garden City 17, 71
Lewis, John 72
Liberal Government (1906) 16,
  17, 18
Lincolnshire 63, 65–6

Lloyd George, David 16, 18,
  21, 27
Lochhead, Richard 35, 83, 86,
  88, 91
Lowe, Philip 27, 101
Lyons Housing Review
  Commission 64–5

M

Marwick, Arthur 22
mass trespass 20–1
McCabe, Tom 98
McDonnell, John 93
Morse, Amyas 98
Munday, Richard and Claire 90
Munton, Richard 3, 10, 56

N

National Audit Office 98
National Farmers' Union (NFU)
  32–3, 99, 101
National Housing Federation
  68, 69, 71
national parks 20, 95–6
National Parks and Access to the
  Countryside Act 1949 20
National Trust 17–18, 28–30,
  47–8
nationalisation 16–17, 19, 22–3
New Domesday Book 52,
  59–60
new towns 17, 70, 71–2
Newby, Howard 4, 7, 102
Nimmo, Alison 44
Norfolk 31, 33, 47, 48–9, 59,
  96–7, 98
Northern Farming Conference
  (2014) 25–6
Northfield Committee 56
Northumberland 39–47, 49,
  51, 52

Northumberland, Duchess of (Jane Percy) 40
Northumberland, 12ᵗʰ Duke of (Ralph Percy) 4, 40–3, 46–7, 49, *50*, 52
Northumberland Estates 39–40, 41–3, 46–7, 52

O

open-field system 14
Open Spaces Society 14
options 65
Orr, David 69
Oxford Farming Conference (2015) 32, 35
Oxfordshire, CLTs 77–8

P

Percy, Jane (Duchess of Northumberland) 40
Percy, Ralph (12th Duke of Northumberland) 4, 40–3, 46–7, 49, *50*, 52
Piketty, Thomas 46
price of land 9–10, 33–4, 63–4, 65, 77–8

R

Raymond, Meurig 101
registration of land 56–60, 88, 91
Return of owners of land, The 52, 59–60
rights of way 20–1, 95–6
Rosselson, Leon 23
Royal Institution of Chartered Surveyors 55

S

Scotland
  and break up of estates 46, 48
  Clearances 81, 82, 86
  community-ownership in 78–9, 88–91
  and Crown Estate 44, *83*
  and foreign landowners 86–7, 87–8
  gulf with English policy 8–9, 35–6, 83–4
  Isle of Eigg Heritage Trust 88–9, *89*, *90*
  and land reforms 8–9, 19, 21–2, 46, 48, 82–6, 90–1
  opponents of reform 8–9, 21, 82, 84–6, 91
  registration of land in 88, 91
  and SNP 8, 21–2, 46, 82–6, 90–1
  and sporting estates 82, 86–7, 91
Scott, Richard (10th Duke of Buccleuch and Queensbury) 4, 8–9, 18–19, *45*, 46, 49, 85
Scottish Field 88
Scottish Land and Estates 84–5
Scottish Land Fund 91
Scottish National Party 8, 21–2, 46, 82–6, 90–1
sea levels, rising 95–9
Second Domesday Book 52, 59–60
self-sufficiency 31, 32–3, 99
Shapps, Grant 75–6
Shieldaig, Wester Ross 90
Smallholdings Act 1890 27
Smiths Gore 33
social housing 67–8
Soil Association 33
SNP 8, 21–2, 46, 82–6, 90–1
Spalding 65, 66
sporting estates 82, 86–7, 91

Stonesfield, Oxfordshire 77–8
Sturgeon, Nicola 8, 21–2, 90–1
subsidies 23, 64, 100–1

T

taxation 18–19, 30, 56, 58,
   69–70, 88, 101–2
tenant farmers 26–30, 47–8
Tenant Farmers' Association
   (TFA) 27–8, 30, 35, 69–70,
   101
Thatcher, Lady (Margaret) 67
tidal surges 96–8
Town and Country Planning
   Act 1947 16, 19–20, 95
Town and Country Planning
   Association 15, 95
Truss, Liz 25–6, 31, 32

W

Walker, John 72
Wallington estate,
   Northumberland *19*, 28–9
Wellcome Trust 34
Westcott-Rudd, Mike 58, 60
Wester Ross 90
Westminster, Duke of (Gerald
   Cavendish Grosvenor) 49–51
Wightman, Andy 82, 86
Williams, Raymond 15
Williams, Tom 23
Winstanley, Gerald 23